The PINK guide to adoption

to adoption

for lesbians and gay men

Nicola Hill

BAAF

ADOPTION & FOSTERING

Published by
British Association for Adoption & Fostering
(BAAF)
Saffron House
6–10 Kirby Street
London EC1N 8TS
www.baaf.org.uk

Charity registration 275689 (England & Wales) and SC039337 (Scotland)

© Nicola Hill, 2009

British Library Cataloguing in Publication Data
A catalogue record for this book is available from the British Library

ISBN 978 1 905664 68 9

Project management by Shaila Shah, Director of Publications, BAAF
Photograph on cover posed by models by istockphoto.com
Designed by Andrew Haig & Associates
Typeset by Fravashi Aga
Printed in Great Britain by The Athenaeum Press
Trade distribution by Turnaround Publisher Services, Unit 3,
Olympia Trading Estate, Coburg Road, London N22 6TZ

BAAF is the leading UK-wide membership organisation for all those concerned with adoption, fostering and child care issues.

Contents

Acknowledgements

I would like to thank Andrew Leary-May for suggesting the idea for the book and finding people to interview; Philip Reay-Smith for reading and commenting on the structure of the book; Laura McCaffrey for reading and commenting on the first draft; and Isabel Atherton, my agent, for finding a publisher. My thanks also to Helen Cosis-Brown, Chris Christophides, Jenifer Lord, Alexandra Conroy-Harris and Katrina Wilson for their helpful comments and input.

Note about the author

Nicola Hill is a writer, specialising in social affairs. She worked as the charities reporter for *The Guardian* and regularly writes about gay issues. Previous publications include *A Very Pink Wedding*, a book about civil partnerships, published by HarperCollins.

Nicola was a referee for her cousin when he was going through the adoption process. She is now a guardian of his adopted child – a boy who has brought great joy to the family. She lives with her partner, Laura, in London.

Foreword

Lots of lesbians and gay men have children. Some have children from previous relationships, some co-parent, some choose to use a surrogate or a donor. And some adopt. Stonewall hears from many lesbians and gay men who have chosen to provide a loving, stable home for some of Britain's most vulnerable children.

Stonewall warmly welcomes this guide for lesbians and gay men who are thinking of adopting children. Stonewall hears from countless lesbian and gay people who fear they may be rejected by adoption agencies, just because of whom they love. As this guide demonstrates, that fear is unfounded.

In 2002, Stonewall lobbied the government to ensure that same-sex couples could apply to adopt children. In 2007, again after interventions from Stonewall, the government reiterated its commitment to gay couples by ensuring that no adoption agency could refuse to consider couples just because they are gay – even religious adoption agencies.

The decision to adopt a child is a significant one. The process of assessment for all potential adopters is rigorous, and rightly so. This guide demonstrates to lesbians and gay men that they *can* apply to adopt children, and that they will be judged solely on their ability to parent.

If you're thinking of adopting, congratulations, and good luck.

Ben Summerskill
Chief Executive
Stonewall

Introduction

History in the making

Gay men and lesbians are making history by becoming some of the first same-sex couples in the UK to adopt children. This book celebrates their pioneering achievements. It tells their stories from first deciding to adopt through to welcoming children into their homes. This book also aims to encourage gay men and lesbians who are thinking of following in their brave footsteps. It contains useful information on research into gay parenting, the legal aspects of adoption, and the steps you need to take in the adoption process and lists useful resources.

An increasing number of gay men and lesbians are deciding to adopt children. In 2006/07, there were 90 same-sex couples in England who adopted. In 2007/8, there were 80. This increase has been helped by a change in the law in England and Wales in 2005, allowing same-sex couples to adopt jointly; prior to that, only one of the same-sex partnership could legally adopt. Scotland's new adoption legislation has similar provisions; in Northern Ireland, new adoption legislation is expected. It is also now against the law in England, Wales and Scotland for local authorities and other adoption agencies to discriminate against prospective adopters because of their sexuality.

These legal changes have encouraged more gay and lesbian couples to approach adoption agencies and equally, agencies are beginning to realise the vast untapped resource of our community. Many gay men and lesbians choose adoption as a first, rather than a last, resort to form a family. This is unlike heterosexual couples, many of whom choose to adopt because they haven't been able to conceive. They often want a baby, whereas same-sex couples seem more willing to adopt sibling groups or older children as a positive choice – a way of having two or three children at once and forming an instant family. For others, a willingness to adopt siblings or older children may be a pragmatic way of moving up the waiting list.

Same-sex couples can sometimes be an ideal match for a child who has been abused by the opposite gender. Children may feel safer, for example, with two women if they have been abused by a man or with two men if their mother has neglected them. Gay men and lesbians will also know what it is like to be in a minority and may have encountered bullying or discrimination, so will be able to help a child who may encounter discrimination on the grounds of being adopted or living with a same-sex couple.

For some gay men and lesbians, adoption is a way of creating a family where both parents are equal, with neither being the biological parent. It also means that the children become exclusively part of your nuclear unit and you do not need to share them with sperm donors or surrogate mothers.

This book

This book brings together, for the first time, information and advice on many aspects of adoption, for lesbians and gay men. The first part of the book takes you through the stages of the adoption process – from deciding if it is the right path for you through to a child living with you. It covers what to expect when you contact an agency, the application form, the preparation course, the home study, the matching process and introductions to children as well as what happens when the children move in. There are helpful checklists, resources and advice. The second part of the book is devoted to interviews with gay men and lesbians – some going through the first stages, some who have recently adopted and others who adopted a few years before the law changed, which allowed couples to adopt jointly.

Please note that this book does not purport to be the definitive guide to adoption in the UK today. For that, readers considering adoption must read *Adopting a Child* (Lord, 2008), published by BAAF. This is a comprehensive guide which explains the law and describes the process and procedures. It is regularly updated and keeps pace with changing requirements. It also lists all the adoption agencies in the UK. Another useful guide is *The Adopter's Handbook* (Salter, 2006), also published by BAAF, which contains information, resources and services for adoptive parents, including lists of useful organisations.

So why *The Pink Guide to Adoption*? What distinguishes this book from the two titles mentioned above is that it focuses exclusively on adoption by lesbians and gay men. While it does offer an overview of the adoption process, it highlights those issues of particular relevance to lesbians and gay men; all quotations and case studies are from lesbians and gay men – both single and in partnerships; throughout, it has a "gay slant"!

Adopting a child or children is one of the biggest decisions in your life. This book will provide a useful companion on your exciting journey.

Note

All names have been changed in the case studies to protect identity. Quotes from the case studies appear throughout the first section of the book. Their full stories are featured in the second half of the book.

WHAT IS ADOPTION?

Adoption is a way of providing a new family for a child who cannot be brought up by their birth family. It is a legal procedure by which the responsibility of parenting is transferred to adoptive parents. Once an adoption order has been granted, all legal ties with the birth parents are terminated and the child becomes a member of the adoptive family.

Legal changes

In England, Wales and Scotland

There have been significant changes in the law recently, which have supported adoption by lesbians and gay men. The Adoption and Children Act 2002, which applies to England and Wales, came into force in 2005. This allowed same-sex couples to adopt *jointly* for the first time. Gay men and lesbians have been adopting children for many years; however, even if they were in a couple, only one of them could apply to adopt. Also since April 2007, lesbian and gay couples cannot be discriminated against by adoption agencies, under the Equality Act (Sexual Orientation Regulations) 2007. Since the end of 2008, this law also applies to adoption agencies that have a religious basis, for example, Catholic charities that provide adoption services.

The Civil Partnership Act 2004, which came into effect in 2005, enabled same-sex couples to obtain legal recognition of their relationship. That a couple have entered into a civil partnership should be taken to demonstrate the same degree of commitment to each other as marriage does for heterosexual men and women.

In Scotland, adoption is covered by the Children (Scotland) Act 1995 and the Adoption and Children (Scotland) Act 2007. The latter allows same-sex couples to adopt, giving them the same parenting rights as heterosexual couples. The Act states that couples who are in a civil partnership or who are living together 'as if civil partners in an enduring family relationship' may adopt.

In Northern Ireland

In Northern Ireland, same-sex couples cannot adopt jointly. A single lesbian or gay man may adopt but it is likely to be harder for single people to adopt than for couples, as is the case in the rest of the UK. The legislation may be reviewed in the future, but this is not imminent. Lesbian and gay couples resident in Northern Ireland could adopt a child in England and Wales, using the Adoption and Children Act 2002, which requires residence in the British Islands.

You can find out more about the law in each country in the UK by visiting www.baaf.org.uk/info/lpp/law/index.shtml.

There are also national minimum standards, regulations and regulatory bodies for adoption agencies in England, Wales, Scotland and Northern Ireland. These have been established and developed in recent years to address shortfalls and variations in performance in meeting the needs of looked after children. These standards overall aim to ensure the provision of more consistent and high quality adoption services which place children at the heart of the adoption process. You can find out more about these on www.baaf.org.uk/info/lpp/agencies/index.shtml.

These bodies can be very useful if you encounter any prejudice or discrimination as they set out the minimum standards. For example, the National Minimum Standards for England and Wales state:

> **Plans for recruitment will specify that people who are interested in becoming adoptive parents will be welcomed without prejudice, will be given clear written information about the preparation, assessment and approval procedure and that they will be treated fairly, openly and with respect throughout the adoption process.**

1

What does the research say?

Current research about gay and lesbian parenting focuses on the outcomes for children raised by gay and lesbian parents, but not necessarily on children who have been adopted. However, it gives you evidence with which to counter any homophobia in your quest to become a parent. To help you combat negativity, the research is described under some of the comments you might hear.

Debunking the myths

Gay men and lesbians won't make good parents

Since 1980, there have been over 25 studies comparing outcomes for children from same-sex and heterosexual households. These have looked at social adjustment, school performance, mental health and emotional behaviour, and have focused on children of all ages. None of them have shown significant differences between the two groups of children. Tasker (2005), for example, found that children with lesbian or gay parents have similar psychosocial outcomes to children of heterosexual parents and their experiences of family life are also similar.

Some of the research has been criticised for being too small-scale or biased. The size of samples will always be a problem as the pool of potential subjects is small and understandably, not everyone wants to volunteer to be studied.

One study, in 2005, tried to overcome the two accusations of bias – that researchers are keen to prove a point and volunteers want to show how good they are as parents. Psychologists at the Universities of Virginia and Arizona, in the USA, published a study of 44 teenagers, growing up in female same-sex households. The families came from a range of income levels and were part of a national family survey, so they weren't volunteering specifically for a study on gay parenting. A team of government researchers carried out the interviews, which covered a wide range of social issues. The results, published in the journal, *Child Development*, found that the children were typical American teenagers, with no significant differences when compared with a similar sample of 44 children growing up in heterosexual families. 'They even reported being more involved at school, in clubs, after-school activities, things like that,' said the report's author, Dr Charlotte Patterson.

According to Patterson (2009), who has reviewed other studies:

> There is no evidence to suggest that lesbian women or gay men are unfit to be parents or that psychosocial development among children of lesbian women or gay men is compromised relative to that among offspring of heterosexual parents. Not a single study has found children of lesbian or gay parents to be disadvantaged in any significant respect relative to children of heterosexual parents. Indeed, the evidence to date suggests that home environments provided by lesbian and gay parents are as likely as those provided by heterosexual parents to support and enable children's psychosocial growth.

A recent report in the USA by a non-partisan research group

(Howard and Freundlich, 2008) concluded that gays and lesbians are an important resource for children awaiting adoption. The report, published by the Evan B. Donaldson Adoption Institute, says there is near 'universal professional consensus' that these applicants should be judged on their qualifications, not sexual orientation. 'The pool of potential adoptive parents must be expanded to keep pace with the growing number of kids in foster care who are legally free for adoption.'

Good parenting is not determined by sexuality, it is about how much time, commitment, love and support you give to your children, as well as setting boundaries and providing a caring structure for their lives. Another riposte to the argument that gay men and lesbians won't make good parents is that most children needing adoption will have been brought into the world by heterosexual parents, who clearly haven't been able to look after their child, for whatever reason, and so it is not sexuality but parenting that matters.

Some studies have shown positive advantages of growing up in a same-sex family. Brooks and Goldberg (2001) studied a group of gay and lesbian adopters, prospective adopters and social workers. They state that:

> Our findings support the notion advanced by findings from these studies that gay men and lesbians actually may have special strengths that make them particularly suited for adoptive and foster parenting. Many participants in our focus group, for example, emphasised how an extended network of family and friends assists them in caring for and providing support to their adopted and foster children. Agency staff mentioned additional strengths of gay and lesbian adoptive and foster parents, including psychological stability, resourcefulness, sensitivity, educational accomplishments, and financial security.

Golombok and Tasker (1996) also found that children brought up in a lesbian household had more open relationships with their mothers and were more secure than their counterparts in heterosexual families.

The children will become gay or lesbian

Evidence from the UK and USA shows that children brought up by same-sex parents are no more likely to grow up gay or lesbian than those brought up in heterosexual families. At least twelve studies have looked at this question and all have found that there is no more likelihood of children of same-sex parents being gay or lesbian than the general population.

For example, Huggins (1989) interviewed 36 teenagers, half had lesbian mothers and the other half had heterosexual mothers. None of the children of lesbians identified as lesbian or gay whereas one of the children of heterosexual mothers did. Bailey (1995) interviewed adult sons of gay fathers and over 90 per cent identified as heterosexual.

If people throw this argument at you, it's always worth pointing out that it's predominantly heterosexual parents that produce gay and lesbian children.

Children will be teased or bullied

Patterson (2009) says:

> **Fears about children of lesbians and gay men being...ostracized by peers, or isolated in single-sex lesbian or gay communities have received no support from the results of existing research.**

One study by Tasker and Golombok (1997) showed that children raised by lesbians were no more likely than the children of heterosexual mothers to experience teasing or bullying.

It is a reality that children may be teased or bullied for having same-sex parents but they may be teased or bullied for wearing glasses, being overweight or too clever. If gay men and lesbians didn't adopt children in case the latter encountered prejudice, you could apply the same rule to, for example, the black and minority ethnic or disabled communities. The fear of homophobic bullying is not a strong enough reason to stop gay men or lesbians adopting. It is homophobic bullying which should be stopped, not adoption by gay men or lesbians. In addition, gay men and lesbians may be in a strong position to help their children deal with prejudice as they may have encountered it themselves.

Barrett and Tasker (2001) reported that most of the adolescents with gay fathers in their study were not open with heterosexual friends about their fathers' sexual orientation. On the other hand, Gartrell and her colleagues (2005) reported that most of the 10-year-olds with lesbian mothers whom they interviewed were open with peers about their families. It is possible that, over the last several years, and in some environments, it has become easier for children to feel comfortable about disclosing that they have non-heterosexual parents.

They will lack male or female role models

In reality, most children, regardless of family structure, will be surrounded by both male and female role models at school, in the community and from amongst family and friends. During the assessment of prospective adopters, social workers ask about the support network to ensure that a child will have male and female role models.

According to Brooks and Goldberg (2001):

> Studies indicated that the gender identity development of children raised by lesbian mothers or gay fathers is consistent with children's biological gender (Golombok

et al, 1983; Green *et al*, 1986; Kirkpatrick *et al*,1981).
Other findings generally show no differences among
children raised by gay or lesbian parents and children
raised by heterosexual parents in their gender-role
behaviour (Golombok *et al*, 1983; Green *et al*, 1986;
Hoeffer, 1981; Kirkpatrick *et al*, 1981).

Another point to make is that a single parent heads 25 per cent of
households in the UK. And so, the children of lesbian or gay parents
are not alone in having a parent or parents of one sex. It is often
stated that children of single mothers, for example, lack male role
models but, as mentioned previously, both male and female role
models are available in the wider family and community.

Gay men won't make good fathers

Scallen (1981) reported no significant differences between 20 gay
fathers and 20 heterosexual fathers in paternal problem solving,
emphasis placed on recreation, and the degree to which autonomy
was encouraged. McCann and Delmonte (2005) state that:

> Research shows that gay fathers try harder to create
> stable home lives and positive relationships than would
> be expected among traditional heterosexual parents
> (Turner *et al*, 1990). Another study highlights that there
> is a more even division of responsibilities for household
> maintenance and child care (Mc Pherson, 1993). It has
> also been suggested that gay fathers may feel
> additional pressures in being more proficient in their
> parenting role, as they may believe that they are being
> more closely scrutinised, due to their sexual preference
> (Bigner and Jacobsen, 1989b).

Mallon (2004), who studied 20 gay men who had become parents,
concluded that:

One of the most enduring impressions that I had of the gay dads whom I interviewed was of their deep commitment to family and parenthood, despite the challenges and frustrations of living in a society that presumes that parenthood is the sole province of heterosexuals.

There is a greater risk of sexual abuse

One of the most insulting accusations people may throw at you is the connection between gay men and paedophilia. A 1994 study on sexual orientation and child abuse found that out of 269 cases of sexually abused children, only two offenders were identified as gay.

Brooks and Goldberg (2001) state that:

Results from general studies on molestation established no correlation between homosexuality and child molestation (Groth and Birnbaum, 1978). In fact, research shows that most child sexual abuse cases involve a heterosexual male abusing a young female (Gebhard et al, 1965; Groth and Birnbaum, 1978; Meiselman, 1978; Patterson, 1992). A recent Child Welfare League of America report revealed that 90 percent of all pedophiles (sic) are heterosexual males (Sullivan, 1995).

Your parents won't approve

It may well be your parents throwing these arguments at you but it is your life and you are the next generation. In fact, participants in Mallon's study (2004) found that parents and families were often more supportive than was first anticipated. Some of the experiences recounted by those in the second part of this book echo this.

Children won't do as well at school

A large, nationally representative sample of children in the USA found that children of same-sex couples are as likely to make normal progress through school as the children of most other family structures. Heterosexual married couples are the family type whose children have the lowest rates of grade retention, according to Michael Rosenfeld (2007).

Hopefully, you won't encounter any prejudice in the adoption process but if you do, make sure you are armed with answers to discriminatory anti-gay statements. This will also help if your children encounter any discrimination.

> Children need good parents, so don't let your worries about society's reaction hinder your desire and ability to give a child a loving, caring home – we've done it, and the reaction, even from strangers, and our kids' church-funded school, has been brilliant!
> *Laurent and Goudarz*

Overview

Fiona Tasker, in her article, 'Lesbian mothers, gay fathers and their children: a review' (2005), states:

> While there is no evidence that children experience difficulties because of being brought up by lesbian or gay parents, it is also important to remember the variation in their experiences. Like children brought up by heterosexual parents, some children in these families will be doing well while others may be currently experiencing problems. Research findings to date indicate that some family processes, such as the effects of parenting stress, parental conflict and parental

mental illness, have similar consequences for children across different types of family form, irrespective of parental sexual orientation.

Tasker calls for more specific research into the outcomes for children who have been adopted by gay men and lesbians. This would further help to combat negative attitudes towards gay men and lesbians adopting children.

In her article with Bellamy (2007), 'Reviewing lesbian and gay adoption and foster care: the developmental outcomes for children' Tasker argues:

Leaving aside the objections some would make on religious grounds, placing children with same-sex couples is likely to remain vulnerable to criticism when evidence on developmental outcomes for children adopted or fostered by lesbians or gay men rests on generalising results from the wider literature on lesbian and gay parenting. The case for further research in this area is compelling.

2

The reality of adoption

Who is being looked after and who is adopted?

There are around 80,000 children being looked after by local authorities in the UK. To give you an idea of the type of children in care, here are some key statistics on looked after children in the UK.

In England

Statistics from England (DCSF, 2008, www.dcsf.gov.uk/rsgateway/DB/SFR/S000810/index.shtml), based on figures in the year up to 31 March 2008, show:

Number of looked after children   59,500
Number of children adopted   3,200
Of the children in public care:
56% are boys

How old are they?
5% are aged under 1
15% are 1–4
17% are 5–9

42% are 10–15
21% are aged 16 and over

Where are they?
71% are in foster homes
11% are in children's homes
8% are living with parents
4% are placed for adoption
6% are placed in other settings

Adoption
Average age at adoption is 3 years and 11 months.
91% of children were adopted by couples and 9% by single people.

In Scotland

Statistics from Scotland (www.scotland.gov.uk/Publications/2008/11/25103230/0), in the year up to 31 March 2008, show the following:

There were 14,886 children in care, an increase of 6% on the previous year.
68% were aged 5–15 with just under half in the 12–15 category
86.7% were white
2% were from minority ethnic backgrounds

In Wales

Statistics for Wales (http://dissemination.dataunitwales.gov.uk) in the year up to 31 March 2008 show the following:

There were 4,635 looked after children
54% were boys
88% were white
42.4% were aged between 10 and 15
4.6% were placed for adoption

The average age at adoption was 3 years and 3 months.
2% of children adopted were under the age of 1
77% were aged between 1 and 4
19% were aged between 5 and 9
1% were aged between 10 and 15
The average time between entry into care and adoption was 2 years and 3 months.

In Northern Ireland

Statistics from Northern Ireland (www.dhsspsni.gov.uk/index/stats_research/stats-cib/stats-cib_pubs.htm) in the year up to 31 March 2006 show the following:

2,433 children were in care
52% were boys
2% were under 1
32% were aged between 5 and 11
57% were living with foster parents
64% children were adopted
The average age at adoption was 4 years and 11 months

The children needing adoption

As you can see from the statistics, there are very few babies needing adoption. Even where families experience difficulties, local authorities try to keep families together and also support single mothers. However, if it is clear that parents cannot keep their child safe and/or the child's wellbeing is under threat, then children get taken into care. And then too, attempts are made to reunite the child with his or her birth family, if possible. If social workers decide that a permanent return home to the birth family is not in the best interests of the child, then adoption will be considered, i.e. adoption is the preferred option when all other options have been exhausted.

There are many reasons why children come into care (also referred to as being "looked after"). Often, it is because one or both parents misuse drugs or alcohol, and have also had other children taken into care. It could also be because of neglect and/or abuse, which could include emotional, physical or sexual abuse, or any combination thereof. Another reason is if a parent is experiencing mental health problems or has chronic health difficulties which make them unable to care for their child properly.

Children who have come into the care system and need adoption, whatever their age, will have experienced the negative impact of their early adverse experiences. For example, a baby taken into care may have Foetal Alcohol Syndrome, as a result of the mother's alcoholism. Toddlers may have experienced abuse or neglect. Slightly older children may have experienced moves between foster families, their birth family, and sometimes extended family. All these children will have suffered the effects of separation and loss in varying degrees.

These traumatic beginnings could result in a range of difficulties for these children, such as attachment disorders, where a child may find it hard to form a secure and trusting relationship with an adult or adults. Some children express their confusion, anxiety and strong emotions by displaying very challenging behaviour; others may experience developmental delay or problems. These children will need to come to terms with their difficult early experiences, and may need therapeutic help to do so.

Not all children who are looked after need adoption. Many will return home while, for others, foster care may be the better option. In the UK, around 4,000 children a year need to be adopted. Many children who need adopting are of school age and over half are in groups of brothers and sisters who need to be placed together.

Some children waiting for adoption are black or from other minority ethnic groups. It is considered best that children be placed with prospective adopters who match their cultural, ethnic and religious profile as closely as possible. The Adoption and Children Act 2002 states that: 'In placing the child for adoption, the adoption agency must give due consideration to the child's religious persuasion, racial origin and cultural and linguistic background'. This guiding principle is also echoed in Scottish legislation.

But this is an area which has provoked a lot of commentary and heated debate. On the one hand, it is accepted that black and minority ethnic children are highly likely to face racism and a parent who shares their heritage would be best placed to support them. Black children also need black adults they can look up to and with whom they can identify positively, as this will help their own identity formation. The experiences of transracially adopted people are a powerful reminder of the complexities for black and minority ethnic children of being raised in a white adoptive family, and the lifelong impact this can have (see Harris (ed), 2006). On the other hand, there is deep concern about the length of time that black and minority ethnic children have to wait until a match is found. It is accepted that such delay can have harmful effects. If, after active family finding, parents who reflect the child's background cannot be found, then it may well be accepted that a wider range of families should be considered. Some children have a very complex and varied background, and it may be impossible to match this exactly.

Some adoption agencies do consider transracial adoption, especially in cases where they feel that the parents will be able to support the child's heritage. There is an example in this book of a white lesbian couple who adopted a black child in London. If you or your partner are black, or from a minority ethnic group, you may stand a greater chance of finding a match more quickly. But even this can prove difficult, especially if your heritage does not match that of any children waiting.

> **This was one of the most frustrating things in the process. While the idea of placing children with parents of the same racial/cultural background makes sense, it is often pushed to an absurd level by social workers.**

> Some children have such unique backgrounds that it is unlikely that any one set of parents could tick all boxes. *Goudarz*

If you are prepared to adopt sibling groups, you are also more likely to find a match. Research suggests that brothers and sisters placed together have a more successful outcome than children adopted on their own (www.bristol.ac.uk/sps/downloads/Hadley/Summary%201%20online.pdf). Children who are adopted in sibling groups can share their experiences and support each other through the adjustment to a new family. Those who are separated from their siblings can experience loss and grief, especially if there is no further contact. There are also advantages to adopting a sibling group as prospective adopters may not have to go through the adoption process more than once, which could be disruptive to the first child you adopt, although, when large sibling groups are placed, sometimes this is done in stages.

Some disabled children are placed for adoption because their parents are not able to care for them. If you have experience of disability, you may be a good match for a disabled child. However, you will need to be prepared to meet the challenges of looking after a child with disabilities. You should get a greater level of support from adoption agencies, over and above financial help, for example, grants for aids and adaptations, if necessary.

Many children who need adoption have learning difficulties. These may be caused by the traumas they have experienced, abuse or neglect or foetal alcohol effects. The learning difficulties may not manifest themselves until later in life.

To give you an idea of the type of children needing adoption, you can ask to see a copy of *Be My Parent* or *Adoption Today* or visit www.bemyparent.org.uk.

Below is a sample of profiles of children on www.bemyparent.org.uk. The actual profiles themselves are much fuller and more comprehensive, and sometimes also accompanied by DVDs. But what is reproduced below will give you an idea of what to expect. The profiles also go on to specify the kind of family that would meet the child's needs and match their ethnic background, the legal status of the child, contact arrangements and preferred area of placement.

CONNOR
Age: 1 year

Connor is an engaging toddler who is keen to be up on his feet and running about. He loves physical contact and will seek his carers out just for cuddles! Connor's birth parents have a history of drug misuse and it is possible that he may have experienced drug withdrawal symptoms. However, he is meeting his developmental milestones.

RHYS AND AYESHA
Age: 5 and 7 years

Rhys and Ayesha are half-brother and sister who share a very close relationship. They have also formed good relationships with their foster carers, with whom they have lived since becoming looked after for two years. Rhys and Ayesha are described by their carers as adorable children with a great sense of humour.

ROBBIE
Age: 3 years

Robbie is a generally happy boy who enjoys his foster family's busy life, and their older children. He loves to run about after his toys. Robbie is delayed in all areas of his development, but is making good progress in his speech and communication. Robbie enjoys making people laugh, smiling and laughing in turn.

SEAN
Age: 8 years

Sean is a bright boy with a thirst for knowledge. He enjoys reading, as well as imaginary play, outdoor activities, watching TV and socialising with adults and peers. Sean has a charming, caring and helpful nature. He can appear confident but, under the surface, he has low self-esteem and requires a lot of praise and encouragement for his achievements.

CHANELLE
Age: 4 years

Chanelle is a bright, bubbly and friendly girl who learns quickly. She enjoys the active outdoor play areas at nursery, as well as the indoor play. Chanelle gets on well with other children and has formed positive relationships with adults, including her foster carers. She is used to the routines in her foster family, and sleeps and eats well.

Adopting from overseas

Information about the process of adopting from overseas should be available from your local authority. The Department for Children, Schools and Families (DCSF) has produced a leaflet which provides an overview of the process for intercountry adoption. The leaflet is aimed at prospective adopters thinking about adopting a child from overseas, and provides further information on the relevant legislation and process. Paper copies of the leaflet can be obtained via the DCSF publications house (Prolog) on 0845 60 222 60 (quoting ref no: DCSF-00809-2008). You can also download it from www.dcsf.gov.uk/intercountryadoption/.

There is also the Intercountry Adoption Centre, which provides useful information on its website at www.icacentre.org.uk/. It has an advice line, runs workshops on adopting from specific countries and offers post-adoption support.

BAAF also has useful information on its website, and publishes a pamphlet, *Intercountry Adoption: Information and guidance*, which describes the intercountry adoption process and basic practical guidance on the procedures and rules surrounding intercountry adoption. Another pamphlet, *Children Adopted from Abroad: Key health and developmental issues*, considers what the child's health needs might be and how to meet them, and covers health assessment, screening and immunisations (see *Useful resources*).

Most countries from which children are adopted and placed abroad do not recognise same-sex couples. This is particularly the case in India and China. If you are thinking of adopting a child from another country, you will need to be approved for intercountry adoption by a local authority or a UK adoption agency that is registered to carry out intercountry adoption assessments. You will need to go through a home study as if you were adopting a child in the UK. In many cases, the local authority will charge for the home study, and this could cost £6,000 or more.

You can only be assessed to adopt from one country during the home study. In many cases, you may need a family connection with the country and you also have to pay the costs connected with the adoption.

The home study report will be sent to the DCSF, the Scottish Executive, the National Assembly for Wales or the Northern Ireland Department of Health, Social Services and Public Safety (DHSSPS) for approval, depending on where you live. The authorities will then send your paperwork to the country you have chosen to adopt from. The authorities in that country will then be responsible for placing a child with you.

When they have found a match, you will have to travel to the country to meet the child. The arrangements for bringing a child back will depend on the country of their origin and will also depend on whether the country has ratified the Hague Convention and whether it is on the UK's list of designated countries, as different procedures apply. You may also have to pay fees to the overseas adoption agency. There are usually solicitor's fees and the cost of translating legal documents, and of course travel and accommodation costs. The process can take between one and three years.

A major issue with adopting from overseas will be helping the child to overcome the challenges of living in a different country, with a different culture, religion and language. There is a high possibility that the child may suffer from deprivation, trauma and institutionalisation. There is a higher risk of unknown health problems if you are adopting a child from a country affected by war or other catastrophes. There may be scant medical records and greater risk of tuberculosis, HIV or hepatitis.

3

Are you ready to adopt?

Who agencies are looking for

Adoption agencies are looking for people with commitment, a good understanding of the challenges of adoption, and who have time and energy to devote to a child. You need to be at least 21 but there is no upper age limit. Some agencies are reluctant to place a child with an adult more than 45 years older than the child. Social workers have a responsibility to place children with adults who are likely to be fit enough to look after a child until they are a young adult. The average age of adopters in the UK is 38. You don't have to be rich or own your own home, but you will need to have a bedroom that the child can sleep in, although an adopted child could share with a child already in your family. However, most agencies prefer there to be at least a two-year gap between any existing child and an adopted child. If you want to adopt a child with special needs but may struggle financially, you may be eligible for financial assistance.

You also don't have to be in a civil partnership. Recent adoption legislation in England and Wales and Scotland allows same-sex couples living together to adopt jointly. However, social workers will expect you to have been together for several years in an established relationship. Single gay men and lesbians can also adopt. Some children benefit from the undivided attention of one adult, so as a single parent you are not necessarily at a disadvantage – it depends if there is a child who needs what you can offer.

All prospective adopters undergo a full medical examination as part of the assessment process. If you have a medical condition or disability, the social worker will have to assess your ability to parent a child until the child reaches adulthood. Agencies will not usually place children, particularly pre-school children, with smokers because of the damaging effects of passive smoking. Social workers will also carefully consider drinking habits, obesity or eating disorders because of the effects on your health and your ability to bring up a child.

If you have been trying to get pregnant, you can get initial information about adoption but adoption agencies will want you to stop any fertility treatment while being assessed for adoption. They will also question you about whether you have overcome the disappointment of not conceiving and may want you to wait for about six months after stopping infertility treatment before starting the adoption assessment. Most agencies want you to be fully committed to just one way of becoming a parent.

Adoption agencies will check whether you have a criminal record. If you have a record, this will not rule you out unless the crime was against children or a sexual offence against an adult. The agency will have discretion to approve adopters who have committed other offences. So it is best to be honest with social workers, as they will consider the nature of the offence and how long ago it took place. The criminal records of other members of the household will also be taken into account.

You don't have to be British but one of you (if in a couple) needs to be "domiciled" or both should be habitually resident in the British Islands. If you have any doubts about where you are "domiciled", you should get legal advice. You need to be prepared to stay in the UK for two to three years as the adoption process may take this long and local authorities may prefer you to be able to stay put for a year or so at least after adoption.

Some agencies have genuinely closed their waiting lists, for example, if they have too many white potential adopters for young children. So if you are refused, check that this is the reason rather than your sexuality. Although some agencies may consider transracial adoption, most try to place children with as close a match as possible to their ethnic and cultural background. The Adoption and Children Act 2002 states: 'In placing the child for adoption, the adoption agency must give due consideration to the child's religious persuasion, racial origin and cultural and linguistic background.'

The aim behind this advice is to provide a supportive home for children with adults who understand their needs and experiences. This will help a child to settle into a new family. However, in some situations, agencies will consider transracial adoption, but will need to be reassured that the child will have access to a multicultural community and role models.

Some faith adoption agencies will try to place children in families with similar faith families. For example, a Jewish adoption agency will seek to place Jewish children with Jewish families. If you are religious, the adoption agency or social worker will discuss with you how this will affect the way you bring up a child.

> The policy of placing children with parents of the same religion might make sense in theory, but in practice this is often a hurdle for gay men. The stance of most religions on homosexuality means that a lot of gay men do not have a strong affiliation with a religious doctrine...Getting past the hurdle of race only to be told that you're not from the right religion is very frustrating.
> *Laurent and Goudarz*

Overall, there is a shortfall of suitable adopters mainly because people have unrealistic expectations of the child they want to adopt, such as wanting to adopt a white baby with no disabilities.

Some people believe that gay men and lesbians are offered children who are the most "difficult to place". It may also be the case that gay men and lesbians are more willing to adopt children with special needs in order to move up the pecking order. There may well be an implication in this that heterosexual couples will be social workers' first choice. Make sure that you only volunteer to adopt children with special needs if that is what *you want to do*, rather than as a way of diluting potentially homophobic attitudes.

How to prepare yourself

BAAF and Adoption UK provide leaflets and information on their websites to help you decide whether adoption is right for you. They will also tell you about the kinds of children who are waiting for new families.

It is a good idea to get some experience of children and child care through volunteering, employment or through spending time with friends, family and colleagues who have children. Many schools and nurseries welcome volunteers to help children read or do other activities. Contact head teachers in the first instance.

> I found a local charity that goes into primary schools and teaches children about environmental issues. I went in and led paper-making sessions with five-year-olds. That was really good and gave me confidence. I also trained to be an independent visitor. It is an adult who has regular contact with a child in care. It is voluntary and you are there to be a friend who is consistent, like a mentor.
> *Simon*

You can also join a gay and lesbian parenting group if there is one nearby, or join online message boards, for example, on Adoption UK, to discuss the process with other gay men and lesbians. The national network New Family Social also has a very active message board on its website. It supports gay men and lesbians throughout the adoption process, linking members with others in their area. (See *Useful resources*.)

You can also read about adoption. Reading about other people's experience of adoption can be very informative as well as inspiring. BAAF has published a few such personal narratives, although none of the titles in this series, published to date, recounts the stories of lesbians or gay men adopting (see *Useful resources*). It is also important to learn about the experiences of adopted people; there have been a few recent publications which tell the adoption story from the adopted person's point of view (again, see *Useful resources*).

Overall, be prepared to be patient. It may only take eight months to the approval stage (around seven months in Scotland), but can take several years to find a suitable match between you and a child.

When you approach an adoption agency, you should be able to demonstrate that you're seriously thinking about the implications of adoption and how you'll meet the child's needs. A social worker or agency will also ask you about your support network.

Questions to ask yourself

Why do you want to adopt?
What experience do you have of child care?
Do you have a good support network?
Do you want to adopt:
- a single child or a sibling group?
- a girl or a boy?

- a child with disabilities or other special needs?
- a child within a specific age range?

What impact will adoption have on:
- your relationship?
- your friends and family?
- other children you may have?
- work?
- leisure-time activities and interests?
- holidays?

What are your views on the following?
- Religion – if you both have a religion, will you focus on one, both or neither?
- Education – do you favour private or state education?
- Discipline – how strict do you think you might be with a child? What are your views on smacking? Will you stick to set boundaries?
- Behaviour – what do you think is important? How will you deal with challenging behaviour?
- Diet – will you bring a child up as a carnivore or vegetarian? Will you take them to fast food outlets?
- Music – will you encourage them to be musical and listen to music?
- Sport – which sports do you enjoy? Will you encourage them to be sporty?
- Other hobbies – what else can you encourage children to do?
- Choosing surnames – will you use one of your surnames? Or both?
- Civil partnership – will you form one, if you haven't already?
- Names – what will you be called? Will one of you be "mummy"/ "daddy" or both of you, or will the child use your first names?

Other questions to ask yourself

How do you feel about contact with birth families?
How will you keep a child's sense of their history and identity alive?
How will you help a child with feelings of loss, anger and grief?
What are your memories of your own childhood?
What have you learned from your parents?
What would your parenting style be?
How would you manage conflict between you over parenting skills?
How would you manage challenging behaviour in children?
What have you done in the past when you have had difficulties?
How much pocket money do you think children should have?
How will you explain sexuality to children?
How will you deal with homophobia?
What is your relationship like with your own parents?
What is your relationship like with friends and family?
Who will be in your support network?

Try to think of other questions under each of these headings. If you are adopting as a couple, spend time comparing your answers with your partner. If you disagree, discuss ways in which you can both compromise to find a united approach.

> You need to talk about issues as a couple beforehand and decide how you are going to handle the process. We had a mutual opt out clause, so if one of us wasn't happy at any stage, we could talk about it and pull out if necessary.
> *Max*
>
> Before you start the adoption process, it is wise to read as much as possible, check out websites, join discussion forums and talk to anyone you know who has adopted a child. (See *Useful resources* for details.)

4

First stages of the adoption process: preparation and assessment

Below is a list of the key stages that you will go through in your journey to adoption. The following two chapters elaborate on each one, and this is brought to life with quotations from people who have already gone through them, whose stories you can read in the second part of this book. There are also useful lists of questions you can ask yourself, and points to consider.

STAGES OF THE ADOPTION PROCESS

Contacting an agency

Initial information session

The preparation course

The home study or assessment

The adoption panel

Introductions

Moving in

The adoption order

Contact arrangements with birth families

Points to consider

Contacting an agency

When you feel you are ready, you need to start contacting adoption agencies. The options are:

- your local authority
- a local authority in another area, whose catchment area includes where you live
- a voluntary adoption agency, e.g. Barnardo's (most voluntary adoption agencies have charitable status)

You can find details of adoption agencies on the BAAF website, www.baaf.org.uk or in the book, *Adopting a Child: A guide for people interested in adoption* (Lord, 2008).

You can also ask to see inspection reports on adoption agencies to assess their efficiency. These are also usually available online. For example, visit www.ofsted.gov.uk for inspection reports on adoption agencies in England; www.carecommission.com in Scotland; www.wales.gov.uk/subisocialpolicy.carestandards/index in Wales; and www.dhsspsni/org.uk in Northern Ireland.

> We visited a voluntary agency and were impressed by their professionalism, their reach (nationwide) and their positive response to us as gay adopters.
> Rachel

> We called a number of local authorities – more than 20 – and only a handful of them seemed willing to take us on. Most of them turned us down saying they did not have children that matched our racial mix, though each rejection made us doubt whether that was being used

as an excuse to stop a gay couple from adopting. Of the three to four that seemed willing to work with us, an adoption charity was definitely the most positive. I remember talking to a social worker who said: 'There is homophobia in the system and so you need someone who is willing to fight for your rights. We most definitely will do everything in our power to ensure that you are not treated any differently.'
Goudarz

When we made our initial enquiry to our local authority's adoption team, the social worker who emailed me responded to my message with a very reassuring tone, assuring me that yes, they would accept an application from a same-sex couple (as that had been my question) and told me that they had made some wonderful placements with same-sex couples over the last few years.
Belinda

Questions to ask all adoption agencies

How many children have you placed with lesbian and gay parents?

Can we meet any of them?

Have your social workers received training about gay and lesbian adopters?

How is gay and lesbian adoption handled in your preparation training course?

Do you use case studies of lesbians and gay men?

How do you handle other people's prejudices in the training group?

What support services does your agency offer during the process and after adoption?

Do you have a support group for gay and lesbian adopters?

> The first local authority used every excuse, except the fact that we were gay. They said there was no way we would ever get a child as our bathroom was downstairs! The next two local authorities who visited us thought this was hilarious and of course said it was no problem. The local authority we chose, which is in the north of England, was fabulous. The only negative thing they said was that because we were a lesbian couple we would never get a baby.
> *Suzie*

> The local authority's reaction was fantastic! Really surprised how supportive they were, especially since we were the first same-sex couple in our area to make an enquiry.
> *Siobhan*

Most people interviewed for this book had positive experiences with local authorities. One social worker said it was more important to assess what a couple could offer a child and to find a good match. She said sexuality should not be an issue.

The National Minimum Standards for local authority adoption services in England and Wales (2003) state that: 'Plans for recruitment will specify that people who are interested in becoming adoptive parents will be welcomed without prejudice.'

In a Good Practice Guide for social workers on assessing lesbian and gay prospective adopters (Mallon and Betts, 2005), the authors say: 'With a national shortfall of adoptive and foster placements, agencies need to ensure that they do not deter lesbian and gay applicants from coming forward as potential carers.' The guide also has a whole chapter devoted to dispelling myths and explaining terminology, so that social workers are better informed about the lesbian and gay community.

Within five working days of contacting an adoption agency, you should receive an information pack – this is a requirement of national minimum standards. The recommended length of time from your formal application up to the time it is considered at an adoption panel meeting, at which they recommend whether or not you should be approved to adopt, is approximately eight months according to guidance for England and Wales under the Adoption and Children Act 2002. For Scotland, the recommended timescale is seven months. In some cases it can take longer, but your agency should keep you informed during every stage of the process.

MINIMUM STANDARDS

There are National Minimum Standards for Adoption set out for adoption agencies in England and Wales. They set out standards applicable to local authority adoption services and voluntary adoption agencies. These are available online at www.dh.gov.uk. They state, for example:

'Written information should be sent to an enquirer within five working days.'

'Follow-up interviews or an invitation for an information meeting should be within two months.'

'The whole process from formal application to decision should take no more than eight months.'

We went to see our local authority for an initial chat. That was really helpful as they were very supportive of same-sex adoption and had placed children with same-sex adopters before.
Simon

Our London borough was recommended to us as gay-friendly, so we thought we'd give them a try, even though they're our own local authority. Many prefer to go with a different local authority so there's no chance of bumping into the birth parents on the high street.
Liam

IF YOU ENCOUNTER DISCRIMINATION

Under the Equality Act (Sexual Orientation Regulations) 2007, adoption agencies in England, Wales and Scotland are not allowed to discriminate against same-sex couples or single gay men or lesbians who wish to adopt. Some Catholic adoption agencies have threatened to stop running their adoption service rather than accept homosexual adopters. In contrast, local authorities and secular adoption agencies will have equal opportunities policies in place and the more enlightened are actively seeking same-sex couples to adopt children, recognising that they can be an important resource. However, some people interviewed for this book have also encountered homophobia among local authority social workers, who sometimes disguise this, for example, by saying they have found a better match, rather than openly displaying prejudice towards you. If you sense that you are being discriminated against, you can complain to the social worker's manager, or the Director of the adoption agency, or even take it further to the Office for Standards in Education (Ofsted). Ofsted does not follow up individual complaints, but will note your complaints for the next time it inspects that agency. General advice on discrimination is available from the Equality and Human Rights Commission helpline on 0845 6046610 (England); 0845 6048810 (Wales); 0845 6045510 (Scotland).

Initial information session

Most adoption agencies will hold an initial information meeting or open day, which will probably include other prospective adopters. The agency will describe how it works and give you the chance to ask any questions. After this, a social worker will arrange a meeting with you at your home or in their office. At this stage, they may say that you don't have enough experience of children or don't seem ready to adopt. If you need to gain more experience of looking after children, you could volunteer at your local school, nursery, hospital or playgroup. You could also baby-sit for other people's children. However, if you and the social worker agree that you are ready to go to the next stage, you should be offered an application form and asked to complete it. This will include your permission for police and health checks and other references.

> Our first meeting with our social worker was great. She had never dealt with a same-sex male couple. She was really good. She said, 'I apologise if I say anything inappropriate and please tell me if I do'.
> *John*

The application form

This asks about your health, reasons for wanting to adopt, financial situation, relationship status and any criminal records. You will have to provide previous addresses for at least the last five years. You will also have to give contact details of referees. The social workers have to follow up all this information to check your financial, medical and criminal records.

A medical examination
The adoption agency will ask you to have a full medical examination with your GP. This will be passed to the agency's medical adviser who will assess if there are any medical reasons why you can't care for a child.

Police check

The adoption agency will run a police check on you and anyone else in your household over the age of 18. This will reveal any spent convictions or cautions. If any of these are for offences against children or sexual offences against adults, you will not be considered suitable for adoption.

Local authority checks

Checks will be made on all your previous addresses.

Financial checks

The adoption agency will need you to show evidence of your income and expenditure. You do not have to be rich but you need to be able to provide a stable environment.

Employment checks

The agency will verify your current employment status and whether there have been any disciplinary proceedings against you. An agency may also gain references from previous employers if you have worked with children.

The preparation course

The next stage is to be invited to attend a preparation course. The preparation course usually consists of four to six sessions, which may be spread over a few weekends or evenings. The course will be with other prospective adopters, both straight and gay. It will involve learning about the children who need adoption and the effect on them of their early experiences. It will also involve talking about your childhood, why you want to adopt, your parenting skills and your expectations, fears and hopes for adoption.

There will be talks from social workers and also from parents who have adopted children. Sometimes agencies also invite birth parents who have given up children for adoption to talk to the group. This can be a harrowing experience for the speaker and for those listening. Adults who were adopted may also share their experiences with the group.

> We really enjoyed it. It was fun and informative and the social workers were great. There was loads of role-play and interaction. They had a fabulous birth mother come in and tell us her story, which was amazing. Also loads of adoptive parents and foster carers.
> *Suzie*

> There were definitely some people who were struggling more on the course because they weren't used to having to interact in groups and share stuff.
> *John*

On the preparation course, topics covered will include the impact of adoption on children, including loss and grief; attachment disorder (finding it difficult to form bonds with people); contact with birth families; managing challenging behaviour; and the support that will be available and how to get it. The course can be emotionally draining as well as inspiring.

> They also expect you to have read quite a lot about issues such as attachment disorders, autism or attention deficit disorder.
> *Chas*

Overall, the course should provide you with an opportunity to ask lots of questions and learn from other people. However, you may be in a different situation to other couples, for whom adoption may be a last resort after having tried fertility treatment, for example.

> It was challenging and had us questioning ourselves whether we really wanted to do it – the answer was always a resounding yes.
> *Rachel*

They want to find out your strengths and weaknesses
and match your strengths to the children's needs, for
example, if you are good at drawing people out who
might be shy or coping calmly when children are angry.
Simon

One of the other couples were Jehovah's Witnesses
and another were salt of the earth East End types,
so we weren't sure how they would react to us as a gay
couple, but they were more than friendly. Everyone got
along very well, although one of the things you are
supposed to demonstrate on the course is tolerance
of others, so we all knew we had to be on our best
behaviour!
Liam

I felt very welcome at the group. There was one other
single applicant – a woman. The social workers were
very accommodating and I never felt excluded as a
single participant.
Richard

ADVICE FROM A LESBIAN SOCIAL WORKER WHO PLACES CHILDREN IN ADOPTIVE FAMILIES

It is essential to go on an adoption preparation course, which
most adoption agencies and local authorities offer for
prospective adopters before starting the home study. This can
be quite a challenge for lesbians and gay men as they meet
other people who want to adopt, over several weeks. You may
be the only gay people on the course so will face the usual
issues regarding coming out and dealing with other people's
attitudes. Many of the straight people on courses will be trying
to adopt because they are childless due to infertility problems.

It is also useful to really engage with the possible backgrounds
of adopted children, for example, they may come from families

where there are issues with drugs, alcohol, violence or mental health. You need to recognise that this makes adoption quite a different sort of parenting commitment to having birth children.

It is very important for prospective adopters to do as much research as possible before approaching an adoption agency or local authority. This will put you in a stronger position and show the agency that you are serious. In my experience, gay and lesbian couples are often more prepared to stretch themselves by taking on more challenging children, perhaps because they haven't tried to have children beforehand. Straight couples who are infertile often want to try to get as near as possible to a birth situation whereas gay couples may be more willing to take on older children or those with more complex needs.

Don't be pushed by an agency to take on a child with complex needs if you feel it is not appropriate for you. However, the chances of getting a child are higher the more flexible you are prepared to be.

Choose your agency or local authority carefully. Meet two or three and ask if they have placed children previously with gay or lesbian parents. Ask about the support they offer post-adoption, for example, courses in attachment or behaviour management. Think about approaching several agencies, even if they are outside your area. In some cases, children need to be adopted outside the area for security reasons.

One of the hardest parts of the adoption process is the waiting. It could happen quickly but could also take years before a match is found. Some agencies also run courses for people who are in the waiting stage.

In my experience, gay and lesbian couples are much more likely to experience discrimination in the matching process even when they have been approved as adopters. It is unlikely that gay people will be the first choice for a young, healthy white child. Sometimes the birth parents may object or it might be prejudice on the part of the social worker. If a child is older, he or she may also object but the agency may be able to work through the issues, such as fear of homophobic bullying, with a child and explain to them the benefits the prospective gay or lesbian couple can offer. If a child is under a court order, a social worker will listen to the birth parents' views but their decision will be based on the child's best interests. If a child is being voluntarily given up for adoption, for example, after a rape, a birth mother may have more of a say. The social worker will have to justify any decisions to the court hearing the adoption case.

Often a gay or lesbian couple's willingness to take on more complexity, such as sibling groups or children with behavioural issues, makes it more likely that children will be placed with them. Discrimination exists in adoption but it is hard to prove, as of course other reasons are usually given for not choosing the gay or lesbian couple.

The process can be hard with the intrusion into your private life and the waiting for a suitable match but it can also be enjoyable. It's a very personal journey.

Choosing referees

You need to provide at least three referees who will be interviewed by social workers. Some agencies require up to eight referees. Try to choose referees who know what you are like with children and are intimate with your home setting, for example, spending Christmas together or other family traditions. At least one of the referees needs to have known you for at least five years. They may also need to know you as a couple. Sometimes agencies will ask to interview previous partners if you brought up a child with them.

The referees usually have to provide a written reference and have a face-to-face meeting with the adoption agency or local authority. The questions can be probing, for example, asking about your attitude to smacking children and how you interact as a couple.

EXAMPLE OF WRITTEN QUESTIONNAIRE SENT TO REFEREES

Here are some questions that may be included.

How long have you known the applicants and in what capacity? How often do you meet?

Do you think in all respects they are suitable people to take a child into their home permanently?

Would the applicants be able to talk to and understand the needs of a child as well as providing adequate physical care and supervision?

If you have a child, would you be happy for the applicant to look after them for a short or long period of time?

Do you know of any circumstances that have made it undesirable or unwise to place a child in the care of the applicants?

EXAMPLE OF FACE-TO-FACE MEETING WITH REFEREES

Here are some questions that may be asked.

How would you describe your relationship with the applicants?

What are the applicants' strengths and areas for development?

Do you think the applicants would abuse a child in any physical or emotional way?

How would the applicants cope in stressful situations?

What support will you offer the applicants?

Would the applicants ask for help if they needed it?

How would the applicants support a child if the child was teased for being adopted or having gay parents?

What is the attitude of the would-be grandparents towards gay parenting?

Prospective Adopters' Report or Form F

The Prospective Adopters' Report (PAR), and its equivalent, Form F in Scotland and Northern Ireland, is an assessment tool used by the majority of agencies in the UK with prospective adopters. It is about 60 pages long and covers all of the areas that must be considered during the assessment, preparation and training of carers, and also provides a standardised way of collecting, analysing and presenting information.

Form PAR/Form F is used to record details about you, for example, your occupation, work experience, ethnicity, religion, lifestyle, interests, experiences and support network. It also asks about your attitudes on areas such as racial discrimination, disability and bringing up adolescents. The social worker will also record information about your partnership, if you are a couple, and how this will affect bringing up a child. The form has a section on parenting skills, including questions about how you manage challenging behaviour, your own experiences of being parented and your understanding of child development. It also covers the type of care you are prepared to offer and details the kind of child or children you want to adopt, for example, age range, gender and number of children. You need to decide with your social worker which type of children you are prepared to adopt.

> You have to state your preferences and stick to that and remind yourself of what you want. For example, we said right from day one that we didn't want to take on children who had been sexually abused or had learning difficulties. That might be right for other people but it's not right for us. We always wanted two boys.
> *John*

> The social worker said it was important to say what
> you do and don't want. The last thing they want is for
> you to take on children that you are not comfortable
> with and for it not to work out. They want you to be
> as open and honest as possible.
> *Chas*

The form also records the type of accommodation you are offering,
for example, a two-bedroom flat in a low-rise building, or a terraced
house. (You don't need to own your home to be an adoptive
parent.) You also have to provide information about the
neighbourhood you live in, for example, the schools, leisure facilities
and public transport options. There is a section about your financial
stability, attitudes towards money and how you will manage when
you are looking after a child. The form is also used to record your
experience with children and your level of competency in different
areas of child care.

The form also covers details of the home visits, the preparation
course and any other training you may have received. The statutory
checks, medical information and references, including a summary
of the face-to-face meeting with referees (although you won't be
allowed to read this) will be attached to your form. The social
worker will follow up any concerns arising from the referees'
statement. Both you and the social worker sign the form. It will
then be passed to the adoption panel.

> As a single parent, I am very keen to adopt a sibling
> group of two, either sex and between three and eight.
> I am particularly keen to take two children, as I think it
> would be more fun for them. They will also have each
> other as support.
> *Richard*

The home study or assessment

After the preparation course, the social worker will carry out a so-called "home study" or assessment. This involves a social worker visiting you at home once or twice a month for about six months. They will ask you searching questions about your lifestyle, relationship and attitudes to parenting. This will include detailed questions about your family background, childhood and current circumstances. For example, they may take you through every year of your life, asking about significant events and the impact they had on you.

> Some parts of the home study were really hard. We had to do a time-line and she wanted a short sentence about a significant thing you could remember in every year. I could remember my brother being born when I was two-and-a-half. To pick up stuff from all those years was hard, like when you split up from your previous partner or when people died. There were happy things as well but seeing it all listed on a piece of paper was really difficult. I started to get angry about things I hadn't thought of in a long time.
> *John*

If you are a couple, the social worker will interview you separately as well as together. Some people find the probing questions intrusive, while others describe the process as valuable, even therapeutic.

> It brought up some interesting stuff in our relationship because it is stuff you wouldn't normally talk about.
> *John*

The social worker is only trying to find out as much as possible about you so they can find a good match and also to help you prepare for adopting a child.

> The home study has been more about getting to know
> us really well so she can match us.
> *Chas*

It is best to be honest with the social worker and admit to weaknesses
as well as strengths. If you are uncomfortable about any questions,
ask why the social worker wants to know the answer. You should
also be honest about any doubts or fears you have at this stage of
the adoption process. If you don't feel comfortable with your social
worker, you may be able to ask for a different one.

> We'd leave each session asking ourselves what was that
> about, what was the social worker trying to ascertain?
> *Rachel*

> Again, we both enjoyed it. We had a fabulous social
> worker. She was more like a friend. She was really open
> and honest so when we were discussing our personal
> life stories she also told us loads about herself so it
> never felt one-way. For us it never felt all that intrusive
> but I can imagine with a more closed social worker it
> must feel like it is.
> *Suzy*

The social worker will ask about previous attempts to have children.
They will also ask about any loss or bereavement you may have
encountered to make sure you are ready to take on a new child in
your life.

> We had some very probing and testing questions in the
> home study about our relationship, sex life and previous
> partners. They also asked how much we drink.
> Sometimes, it was more like a therapy session.
> *Max*

The social worker will also want to assess your home from a health
and safety perspective, for example, checking what adjustments you

may need to make to ensure that cupboards or staircases are safe, particularly if you are hoping to adopt a young child. They will also want to assess the sleeping arrangements for the child or children and find out what space you have available for the child to play in. The social worker will want to know how you will manage childcare arrangements if you both work.

Remember that the home study period is also a time for you to continuously reflect on what you learn about adoption, but also about yourselves. It is a chance for you to ask questions and make sure you are really ready for adoption.

> Be honest with yourself and be honest with the social workers. Social workers make a living off reading people, and if they think you're hiding something, they'll delay the process until they're satisfied that you're not a liability.
> *Goudarz and Laurent*

Helen Cosis-Brown and Christine Cocker (2008), in their article 'Lesbian and gay fostering and adoption: out of the closet, into the mainstream?' state:

> Initially, it is clear that the sexuality of applicants should have little bearing on the outcome of recruitment and assessment. However, this is not to say that an applicant's sexuality is unimportant, but rather that there are other aspects of an individual which are equally or more significant. (p 19)

The article also quotes Brown (1991), who argues that assessments of lesbian and gay applicants should cover five elements:

1. The individual's experience of their homosexuality (their own and their families' response historically);
2. How confident they feel in relation to their sexuality and how comfortable they are as lesbians and gay men;

3. How homophobia and heterosexism have impinged on their lives, how they feel they dealt with this and what coping devices they use;

4. Their present relationships – sexual, emotional, supportive, family, etc – and how they negotiate homophobia within close relationships (e.g. with siblings);

5. Transitions to parenthood – making links with the local community regarding child care resources and contact arrangements with birth family members of adopted children.

Questions you might be asked during the home study

About yourself

What bereavement or other losses have you suffered?

Have you explored other ways of having children?

What is your attitude towards disability?

What impact did culture and religion have on your upbringing?

How will that impact on a child?

What effect could unemployment have on your life?

What are your strengths and weaknesses?

About your lifestyle

What are your drinking, smoking and drug habits?

How do you spend your leisure time?

What sort of people do you socialise with?

Is your diet balanced?

About your relationships

What are the strengths and weaknesses of your relationship with each other?

What were your previous relationships like?

How do you make decisions as a couple?

What are your long-term plans together?

Have you thought about what would happen if you separated?

How do you think adoption will affect your relationship?

About coming out and dealing with homophobia

When did you come out?

Are you "out" to your family, friends, at work, etc?

What was the reaction of family, friends, colleagues? Are they supportive?

How have you dealt with homophobia in the past?

How might you deal with it in the future, for example, if the birth parents of your child or parents of other school children seem homophobic?

How will you deal with homophobia that your child might encounter?

About bringing up children

What is your experience with children?

How will you discuss your sexual orientation with a child?

How would you handle sex education?

What impact will a child have on this relationship?

How will you cope if a child becomes more attached to one of you than the other or tries to play you off against each other?

How will you help a child deal with issues of loss, grief or anger?

If you are capable of looking after a child with a disability, how will this affect your life?

How will you encourage your child to participate in clubs or sports or other activities?

How will you develop a child's self-esteem?

What are your attitudes towards discipline?

What is your understanding of Britain as a multicultural society and how can children be educated to take a positive view of such a society?

How will you manage caring for the child after school/playgroup, and in school holidays? Will one of you take leave? Which one?

It was good to talk about our plans for the future and to reflect on the past. You quite often forget the good things that have happened in the past but I remembered friendships I formed as a child and how I used to play. It helped me to get into the framework of

looking at things from a child's perspective.
Raymond

An experienced and competent worker should inquire
about the prospective parents' lifestyle but should not
over-emphasise the lesbian or gay issues.
Mallon and Betts (2005)

After the home study, the social worker will complete the
Prospective Adopters' Report/Form F with their recommendations.
You will see all the sections of the form apart from the referees'
statements and medical reports and you can agree it or mark any
aspects you don't agree with. If you are unhappy about anything in
the report, you have ten days to comment. If you and the social
worker cannot resolve any issues that you are not happy about, this
will be of concern to the adoption panel. However, you can put your
comments in writing and these can be added to the report. Both
you and the social worker sign the form. It will then be passed to
the adoption panel.

The adoption panel

The PAR/Form F will be sent to the adoption panel in advance of the
meeting. The panel is made up of around ten people; a couple of
other people may be present, for example, a legal adviser and an
agency adviser.

Panels include:

- a chairperson, who has experience of adoption but who is
  independent of the adoption agency
- two senior social workers, with experience of adoption
- a member of the management committee (for a voluntary
  adoption agency)
- a local councillor (for a local authority)
- a medical adviser

- three independent people who are not members or employees of the agency – they may have been adopted, be adopters or have a general interest in adoption.

There are regulations about the membership of panels that differ between England, Wales and Scotland but regardless of where they are located within the UK, panels are a selected group of people who come together to make recommendations to the adoption agency about the suitability of an applicant.

You will be invited to attend the adoption panel, but there is no compulsion to attend. This will involve answering questions during a section of the meeting for about 10 to 20 minutes. The panel will be trying to assess whether you will make good parents. They will have a copy of your PAR/Form F, but will need to ask about anything which seems unclear or about which they need more information.

> The adoption panel felt much more unnerving than we had expected. Perhaps it was the realisation that so much was riding on it, or just the experience of having 12 strangers peering down a table at you, asking you questions that could determine the rest of your life!
> *Goudarz and Laurent*

> I was a bit worried to start with, thinking should I say what they want to hear...but in the end it's best to be honest. I wanted them to approve us for who we are.
> *Raymond*

They will want to know about your expectations of adoption and whether you understand the emotional needs of the child, particularly in dealing with separation and loss. They may also ask about your views about the birth parents and attitudes towards contact.

In theory, they are not supposed to ask you anything that they wouldn't ask a heterosexual couple. However, they may ask about your network of friends and family, including positive role models of the opposite gender to you. They may also ask how you deal with discrimination. The panel will pick up on any queries they have from your answers on the PAR or Form F. The panel will also interview your social worker separately.

> Through all of this, we didn't think there was any homophobia until right at the end, when we had to meet the social worker's line manager just before we went to panel and that was really uncomfortable. She kept saying 'people like you'...and there were big pauses. It's difficult because you don't want to rock the boat or complain because you think they will shove you to the back of the queue or say no.
> *John*

The panel will make a recommendation to the adoption agency to approve you or not as suitable to adopt. They may also give advice on numbers of children, age, gender, etc, that might be suitable for you, but this is only *advice*, and need not restrict the eventual choice of child placed.

> It didn't last very long and almost as soon as we left the room, the head of the panel followed us out to tell us we'd been approved. It was a life changing moment and Chris, our social worker, and I hugged each other.
> *Liam*

It is unlikely that you will get to this stage if the adoption agency doesn't think you stand a good chance of being recommended for approval by the panel. The final decision about your suitability still rests with the adoption agency. You should be told within seven working days what the decision is.

> It was bloody scary – we arrived at the Civic Centre, a big cold place, and sat in the corridor for what felt like an eternity. We then went into a room to be faced by

10 people. They went through our form and then asked us to leave the room. They then asked us back in and posed a couple of questions (the inevitable male role model question) and asked us to leave again. They called us back in and said it was a unanimous yes...
I then burst into tears!
Suzy

What happens if the agency proposes not to approve you?

If the agency proposes not to approve you, you have 40 working days to challenge this. You can appeal either to the agency or the Independent Review Mechanism (IRM) but not both. The IRM operates in England and is run by BAAF on behalf of the Department for Children, Schools and Families. It is a review process, conducted by an independent panel, which prospective adopters can use when they have been told that their adoption agency does not propose to approve them as suitable to adopt a child. The Welsh Assembly runs a similar system for people who have not been approved by an adoption panel in Wales. The IRM panel's recommendation goes back to the agency, which then makes the final decision. In Scotland, there is a "reconsideration" procedure for applicants. People who have been rejected by one agency can apply to another.

You may feel the agency has rejected you on the grounds of your sexuality. You may also believe that you are not approved for younger children or babies because the panel would prefer to give priority to heterosexual couples. However, some couples have reported that other excuses are being used to mask what they believe is homophobia. This is more subtle and harder to prove. You should ask the agency to make it very clear why any particular decision has been made.

Finding children – the matching process

Once you have been approved, you and your social worker can start looking for a potential match. This means a child or children who need what you can offer. Initially, the social worker will see if there are any children in their local authority or other agencies they work with, for example, in a consortium arrangement, in which agencies "pool" their children. Some local authorities ask you to wait for three months before applying to adopt children outside of their area. If this isn't the case, you can ask to be put on the Adoption Register if you live in England and Wales (see box). This is operated by BAAF. You can also look through magazines such as *Be My Parent* or *Children Who Wait* or websites such as www.bemyparent. org.uk to find a child who may need what you can offer. Every month, an average of 1,200 prospective adopters enquire about children featured in *Be My Parent*.

THE ADOPTION REGISTER

This is a database of children who have not been able to be placed by their local authority, and of approved prospective adopters who are waiting to be matched. A team of staff look at the database to see if they can identify potential matches. Agencies can refer approved adopters to the Adoption Register and will usually do this if it seems as if the adopters won't be matched quickly with a child in their own area. Agencies must refer adopters to the Register three months after they have been approved if a match is not being actively pursued; in such cases, prospective adopters can put themselves forward.

Once the details of a family have been recorded on the Register, a search is undertaken to identify a child who matches the family's approval profile. Relevant details are sent to the child's social worker, who will consider any proposed link. Information about any family on the Register can be sent out up to five times to different social workers to consider a link; if none of these is pursued, the family's details are again made available to enable further searches and for links to be made with other children.

If the child's social worker thinks you might be a good match, you will be sent written information about the child. If you want to proceed, you will be invited to meet the child's social worker for an initial discussion. The social worker will assess the child's and your needs for adoption support services. You will also discuss plans for any contact with the birth or foster family.

> It is a learning process, and we are working out how to filter the information more efficiently. It is hard to reject children but you have to be realistic, you have to weigh up what the child needs and what you can offer.
> *Raymond*

Your social worker should help you consider all the information provided to assess whether you will be a good match. Always keep in mind the needs of the child and how you will be able to meet them. For example, if the child is described as very withdrawn, think about how you may be able to help, based on previous experience or your personality. If the child has any therapeutic needs, find out about any service provision which the agency may be able to offer, and what may be available in your area.

> Four social workers came from the north to see us twice and on a practical level you are thinking they must be keen. But when we started to know more about the children, we knew it wasn't right for us and we had to say no. I know two people who said no twice during matching, which was really hard, really heartbreaking. You have to watch out for social workers glossing over details because they are desperate to place children.
> *John*

The child's social worker may be considering other potential adopters for a particular child, so bear this in mind and try not to get too excited in case they don't choose to place the child with you. If the social worker decides you are the best match, then you will be given a copy of the the child's assessment report (see box).

THE CHILD'S ASSESSMENT REPORT

Previously, the child's assessment report was known as Form E throughout the UK. With the advent of devolution and legislative changes, this form is called the Child's Permanence Report in England; Child's Adoption Assessment Report in Wales; and Form E in both Scotland and Northern Ireland. Although there might be slight differences between the forms, essentially they collect information about the child and the child's history to provide a comprehensive picture of the child.

This report is an essential tool in enabling the adoption agency to plan for the future life of a child. Qualified social workers undertake this assessment, and the information collected on the form is essential to prospective adopters when first approached by the agency about a particular child; and is used by adoption panels to recommend whether the child should be placed for adoption, as well as with which prospective adopters. The assessment report provides information about the child, including his or her family history, any known abuse or neglect and health record. It will also detail any special needs and whether the child has reached normal developmental milestones or not. Sometimes people find such reports very distressing, others have found them frustrating because they are out of date and yet others have said they didn't provide enough information. You may want clarification of some of the information in the report.

After reading the report, you will also meet key people in the child's life such as teachers, foster carers and doctors. They will be able to tell you more about the child and hopefully, give you some photos.

The foster parents weren't too sure about us adopting the children to start with but they were fine once they met us and we explained how we would look after the children.
Max

We met the boys' teachers and they couldn't have been more positive about them. The headmistress was nearly in tears at the thought of losing them. We came away from that thinking thank God, that was a big breakthrough.
John

If you want to proceed at this stage, and the social workers agree, the child's social worker will prepare an adoption placement report and an accompanying adoption support plan (if in England and Wales). This should cover the plans for adoption and any support you or the child may need. You have ten days to consider this. Arrangements elsewhere in the UK are broadly similar.

This report will then be sent to an adoption panel in the child's local authority. They will also see your Form PAR/Form F. You may be invited to attend the panel meeting where they will ask questions about why you want to adopt this particular child or children. They will then make a recommendation to the child's local authority about the suitability of the match.

Our match happened within a week of approval, very obviously we were considered prior to that date. The match was perfect. The boys are everything we could have dreamed of and more. They are brothers aged two and five, with dual heritage and no disabilities.
Siobhan

It was our first experience outside of the super-efficient workings of the adoption charity and inside the super-inefficient world of local authority social services. We'd find children we thought were a good match in *Be My Parent* and *Children Who Wait*, and send our one-page profile to the family-finders, and then wait weeks to hear back. We felt like it was beyond ridiculous that anyone could take three weeks to read one page and decide whether or not we were to be considered. Our social worker always told me, 'The right child for you is out there. You just need to wait for the time when it is meant to be.'

Goudarz and Laurent

5

The next stages of the adoption process: introductions and moving in

If the panel agrees that you could adopt the child or children, the child's social worker will devise a plan for introductions. You will need to compile a DVD or photo album for the child ahead of the introductions so they can see what you look like and how you live. For example, people take photos or a video of themselves, their home, pets, the child's bedroom and any outdoor space.

> We had prepared a book for the children with some photographs of the two of us, in regular everyday clothes, with simple texts like "This is where Papa cooks" or "This is where Daddy works". As soon as we passed the matching panel, the foster carer told the children about us, and showed them these photographs and a simple video of us saying hello. So, by the time we actually met, both adopters and adoptees knew of each other to quite a large extent. This didn't stop us from being very nervous: I remember holding my partner's hand on the way to meeting the boys and thinking 'This is the start of a new chapter in our life'.
> *Goudarz*

The introductions involve meeting the child on a regular basis for up to eight weeks. In some cases, you could meet the child every day for two weeks and each visit will be longer, for example, you may start with a one-hour visit in the child's foster home and build up towards spending the day together. The child may also visit your home and stay overnight on a subsequent visit. Some people also visit the child's school and meet some of their friends. The length of time taken will vary, depending on the child's age, needs, and where he or she lives.

> That first day when you are sitting on their sofa and they say, 'We'll go and get your children', is really surreal. And they come trotting round the corner. We had seen loads of photos and a DVD but to actually see them in the flesh was amazing.
> *John*

> It was very emotional and extremely nerve-racking. The foster carers and social workers were looking at us playing with the children, which was such an alien feeling. We had three long weeks of introductions, which we felt was too long and involved loads of travelling.
> *Siobhan*

> We had this mad two weeks when we did loads of stuff with them that they had never done before like going to the beach, the zoo and the cinema. They weren't used to having two people totally focused on them. It was like a massive holiday for them but at the same time they had to go back to the foster home where there were three other foster children.
> *John*

This is usually a very emotional time for everyone involved. Children may be very wary of you and be uncertain about leaving their friends, foster family and school. Others may be delighted by the attention. It can also be tricky if there are other children in the foster home who are not being adopted, as they may feel jealous.

> Our first meeting was wonderful. We went with the foster carer and collected him from nursery. He'd been shown our photo book and DVD in advance and the foster carer, a woman in her sixties, had prepared him well for his two mummies. On that first meeting, we left the nursery and he took my hand and we've not looked back.
> *Rachel*

If, at this stage, you are not sure it is a good match, you must discuss your concerns with your social worker. After the introductions, you will have another meeting with the child's social worker and other key people in the child's life, to discuss the placement date and the details of the adoption placement plan. This will include arrangements to be made with schools, doctor's surgeries and the support you and the child need and any contact arrangements with the birth and foster family. You will be issued with a matching certificate, which you can use to show your employer in order to get adoption pay and leave.

Moving in

This usually happens swiftly, so the children's lives are less disrupted by long delays. They will usually bring all their clothes and toys with them. They will also bring a life story book that the social worker and/or foster carer have prepared, with the help of the child, if they are old enough. This will have information about the child's family, how the child came to be adopted and a life history. Life story work can help children begin to accept their past, difficult as it may be, and move forwards positively into the future. You can help your child to continue to develop and add to their life story book.

> The very first morning the boys woke up at home, we

saw that they were developing chickenpox...a real
baptism by fire! So the first week was just spent nursing
them. In a way this helped us bond, as it showed them
we were there for them and would take care of their
health. For the first few weeks, we really let nobody
from the extended family and/or friends come to visit
us. This allowed the boys to really understand the
dynamics of their new family and not swamp them with
new faces. Everybody understood and respected our
need for privacy during those initial weeks.
Laurent

You may also get some financial help from the adoption agency to
buy basic items such as a bed, desk or car seat. This is sometimes
known as a "settling in" grant. Some agencies will contribute more
if you have adopted a sibling group or children with special needs.
You can request financial support at any stage after you have
adopted a child but it may well be means-tested.

Don't underestimate how difficult it is on the day you
take them from the foster parents' house. You get
swept along in those introductions and everything is
going well and then suddenly we had to turn up at
ten o'clock on a Wednesday morning. They'd had a big
leaving do the night before, friends from school had
come, and the sofa was full of presents. Everybody was
standing around – the social worker, the foster mum
and dad and us – and we had to put them in the car.
Jack had been fine up to that point, hadn't had a
tantrum and then suddenly he was upstairs in the
house, saying,'You are making me move again...I'm
losing my friends...I don't understand my life...This isn't
fair, everybody just leaves me'. We were all crying.
John

When they first moved in, my partner and I had a
de-briefing every night about what the children were

doing, how we were reacting, did we do it right. We went into a lot of detail but it seemed necessary. It is a big learning experience and you will get things wrong, you just have to go on your instincts.
Max

Statutory Adoption Pay (SAP) and adoption leave

If you are adopting as a couple, one of you needs to opt to be the primary carer so that your employer or the State can pay SAP. Both male and female employees are entitled to SAP and adoption leave. This is paid for a maximum of 39 weeks (this recently went up from 26 weeks). Adoption leave is available for 52 weeks but only the first 39 weeks are covered by SAP. To qualify for SAP and adoption leave, you need to have been employed continuously for 26 weeks. You will need to provide written evidence that you are adopting a child. If you are adopting as a couple, the other partner will get "paternity pay", which is two weeks' paid leave. This is available to male and female adoptive parents. Again, you must have been in continuous employment for 26 weeks to be eligible.

SAP is a minimum and some employers, for example, many local authorities, health trusts and government departments, give much more generous adoption pay. It may be worth comparing each other's employer's adoption leave policy (if you are a couple) and take this into account as part of deciding which of you will be the primary carer.

When I left work, I said I'd rather keep it low key in case it breaks down or goes wrong. But of course as soon as they advertised my job for adoption leave, the whole office went mad. They gave me loads of vouchers, presents and cards. My boss gave a speech in tears.
John

Post-adoption support

The Adoption and Children Act 2002 and the Adoption and
Children (Scotland) Act 2007 place a duty on local authorities to
carry out an assessment of the need for post-adoption support
services. Your social worker should draw up a plan of support for
you and the child. This may include respite care, therapeutic services
or educational support. The child's social worker will visit you in the
first week and at least once a week until the first review takes place
after four weeks. The social worker will also conduct statutory
reviews after four weeks, three months and then on a six-monthly
basis until the adoption order is granted. The visits and reviews are
supposed to be supportive rather than invasive, to check how you
are settling in to being a family together.

> **At the start of the settling-in process, we had to deal
> with more challenging behaviour, mostly because the
> boys didn't really know where our boundaries were,
> and kept testing how far they could go. But this settled
> down quickly with clear rules.**
> *Goudarz*

Children may have mixed feelings about being adopted. They may
be angry but also relieved; they may miss their foster family, but be
pleased that their adoptive family will be their family for life. Moving
home is stressful for anybody at the best of times so, for a child
who may have already moved too many times, moving in with you
may be another unsettling experience. For some children, it may
take a while before they believe that they will not need to move
again. During the initial settling-in period, the child will need a
lot of help, including with a new family, a new home, a new
neighbourhood, a new school…and it may take a while before
your child feels safe and secure.

This settling-in period may be difficult for you too. Combined with
the excitement of "your" child moving in, there will be an anxiety
that all goes well. As the child is getting used to you, you will spend

the time getting to know your child, and adjusting to the new family unit that now exists.

This can be a demanding time for everyone involved. If you need help, you should ask for it.

There are post-adoption centres across the UK, which run events on issues such as managing challenging behaviour. There are also a number of post-adoption courses that you might be interested in attending. Adoption UK runs a training programme, which has modules on placement, contact, education and telling life stories. It is a good idea to find support groups in your area – some may be for lesbian and gay parents or for all adopters. They often provide fun days out for adoptive families, group therapy sessions and forums for exchanging information. (See *Useful resources*.)

The adoption order

An adoption order is granted in a court of law. The order cannot be made until the child has been living with you for ten weeks, If a child has been placed by an agency. (Other periods apply for step-parents, private adoptions and local authority foster carers and there is also a requirement to give notice to the local authority three months before making the application.)

The birth parents do not have to agree to an adoption order if the court decides that their consent should be dispensed with because either the parent cannot be found, is incapable of giving consent or the child's welfare requires it. The birth parents cannot oppose the making of an adoption order without the court's leave if they have previously consented or the court has made a placement order. Leave will only be granted if there has been a significant change of circumstances.

In England and Wales, you apply for an adoption order through your local Magistrates' Family Proceedings Court or the County

Court. In Scotland, you lodge a petition with the Sheriff Court or the Court of Session. In Northern Ireland, you apply to the County Court or to the High Court.

Before the court hearing, the social worker, who placed the child with you, prepares a report. This gives the court information about the child, their birth family and your circumstances. It will also detail how the settling-in period has gone. The social worker will also talk to the birth parents to make sure they understand the implications of adoption.

In England and Wales, a local authority has to have the consent of both birth parents, if they both have parental responsibility (whether married or not) or of guardians if parents are dead, or they must have a placement order, granted by a court, before they can place a child with you. So it will only be in exceptional circumstances that birth parents can contest an adoption. In Scotland, if birth parents don't agree, you have to ask the court to override their objection.

The courts will consider the best interests of the child and whether the birth parents are being unreasonable in their objection. In the vast majority of cases, these issues will have been sorted out before you get to court.

The court hearing usually lasts half an hour and you will be asked a few questions by the judge or magistrate. The judge may also ask your child some questions, if they are old enough. In Scotland, any child aged 12 or over is asked if they agree to the adoption. In many cases, the adoption hearing will be conducted in an informal way, with children even trying on the judge's wig! The court will make a decision that day and you will be told immediately.

An adoption order transfers complete and permanent parental responsibility to the adoptive parents. Your child will receive a new short certificate which replaces the birth certificate and the law now recognises the adopted child as having the same status in the family as would a child born into a family.

Contact arrangements with birth families

There is no set rule regarding contact and each child's needs vary. The child's best interests will be the deciding factor although the birth family and adoptive parents will be able to express their views. Contact can range from an annual exchange of letters via the adoption agency to meeting siblings, parents or grandparents on a regular basis. Sometimes letters and photos are exchanged between the child and the birth family – this is called "letterbox contact". Foster carers may also request ongoing contact. Contact arrangements can be altered as a child gets older, according to their needs and wishes.

We lobbied our social workers really hard to be able to meet with the birth mother. The main reason was that we had very limited information on her, in particular, no photographs of her to show the boys when they grow up. It was again a meeting that made us both very anxious beforehand, but will prove valuable in time. We were able to get pictures of her, cards that she wants us to give them on their 16th birthdays, a short video saying that she wants them to come and meet her when they grow up, an explanation of who chose their names, a detailed run-down on diseases running in the family, etc. We also got a lot more clarification on the circumstances surrounding their being placed in care: we found that there were some substantial errors in the records held by social services.

We also met with their half-siblings. This was very touching, in particular, seeing how their half-brother resembles our older son. There again, those pictures and clarifications on the family background have proved much more illuminating than any paperwork could. We would recommend all adopters to go for contact with the birth family whenever feasible, despite the stress and anxiety this might cause.
Goudarz

Points to consider

Reaction of family

Some people have had unfortunate experiences of family members saying they won't recognise the adopted child as part of the family. Others have shown their disapproval at the prospect of gay or lesbian couples having a family. For some people, the notion of lesbians and gay men raising children seems to be taboo, even if they have been accepting of your sexuality and relationship up to this point.

You need to be prepared for this kind of negativity and decide how you are going to deal with it. The child should not experience this rejection so you may need to decide not to have anything to do with family members who reject you. Remember that attitudes can and do change.

> If there is any hostility in the family, the children have to come first.
> *Max*

What to call you

One issue is whether or not to both be called Mummy, Daddy or whatever term you choose or for one of you to be called by your first name. Whatever you choose, there should be an easy way to distinguish between you, for example, Mummy Barbara and Mummy Sarah or Dad and Pa.

In terms of surnames, you may want to opt to both have the same surname as each other, which you can do if you have formed a civil partnership. This can be one of your surnames, or a new surname for you both. You can then give this to the child, if they are happy to change their surname. Another option is to have a double-barrelled version of both your names. In this case, you will both have to change your names. Name change is easy to do and you should avoid lawyers or agencies which try to charge substantial fees (see Change of Name on the CAB website – www.adviceguide. org.uk/index/family_parent/family/change_of_name.htm). When an adoption order is made, you choose the name of the child which will appear on the adoption certificate.

Contact and degree of involvement with birth and foster family

Social workers are generally keen to keep some form of contact between the child and their birth and/or foster carers, grandparents or siblings. However, this can cause distress to the children and you as the new adoptive parents. For example, if a child has been neglected or abused, it may be very difficult to see a birth family member again. If a child had a very good relationship with a foster carer, this can also cause confusion in their lives when they visit them. The child may also show more affection for their foster carer in the early stages and want to move back in with them. This is not easy when you may be trying very hard to provide a stable environment, which is disrupted every time the child has to visit birth or foster parents. There may also be homophobic reactions from birth or foster parents that you have to deal with. If you are unhappy about contact arrangements, discuss it with your social worker. Some people have refused contact and the social worker has agreed to this.

There can, however, be great benefits for a child to maintain contact with their birth family, so that he or she feels a sense of continuity and identity. Sometimes, healthy relationships can be maintained with birth grandparents, who can give a child a strong sense of their own history. A child may have a range of half- or step-siblings and contact can be important to establish a sense of his or her extended family.

Jack says, 'I'm going to find her when I'm 18'. Whereas Colin says, 'No way, I'm never going to see her again', because he remembers mummy drunk, on drugs, having other men in the house, daddy dying. He remembers all of that.
John

We have had annual letterbox contact but until last week we hadn't heard anything back. It was great to receive our first letter and to know the birth mother is thinking about our little one.
Suzy

Challenging behaviour

You are likely to experience some challenging behaviour when a child first moves in as he or she will be testing the boundaries, playing one parent off against the other, and struggling to find their place in a new family. A child may also have difficulty trusting you or feeling secure because of prior negative experiences of adults. An older child may say she or he doesn't want to settle with you and may blame this on your sexuality but you need to unpick this as this could be an excuse and there may be something deeper underlying this.

Children may also express their grief at the loss of their foster carers or birth parents. This may be expressed in anger or by becoming withdrawn. They may also self-harm. You need to be very watchful for signs of self-harm and be prepared to talk to the child, allowing them to express anger and hurt at being adopted. Talk to your social worker and arrange therapy, if you or your child needs help.

A child may also regress, as this may be the first time they are being offered the love that they didn't get as a younger child. Be prepared for a child wanting to be treated like a baby or toddler and make sure they feel comforted through these stages.

> The children tried to polarise us into good daddy, bad daddy. Good daddy who buys things, bad daddy who makes us tidy up. They tried to provoke responses they have had before; for example, they had been smacked by previous carers, so behaved badly to try to provoke us into doing the same. Previous carers had also shown favouritism between them, so we had to be religiously fair when buying anything for them or handing out praise to undo that pattern.
> *Max*

Difficulties in your relationships

Adoption may cause a lot of stress in your relationship as a couple or in your relationships with others. You may also feel under pressure to prove how good you are as parents. The children may also play one off against the other to test your boundaries. Be prepared to talk to each other constantly and, if necessary, seek counselling for you and the children to get through difficult times.

> Our relationship is stronger, although our sex life has suffered. We need to find ways to spend more time together alone.
> *Rachel*

Coming out all over again

Having children will force you into many situations, where there may not be many gay parents and you will have to "come out" again. For example, at the doctor's, schools, swimming lessons, nursery. Often children will out you before you get the chance. Younger children, who tend to be very accepting and matter-of-fact, will quite often announce that this is Daddy James, and this is Daddy Mark.

It is important that you don't make the children hide your sexuality but you may want to let them know that not everyone may accept the fact that you are lesbian or gay. You will need to learn how to manage such situations and teach your child how to manage them too. Older children may be conscious of homophobic bullying or teasing and choose to hide your sexuality. Don't make this an issue – it is their life and they need to manage it. Over time, this could change.

> I think the main tension any children experience is the difference between home culture and school culture. At home being gay is fine and we talk about it quite openly but at school, gay is used as a term of abuse.
> *Max*

It is better to be open with the children about your sexuality so that they don't hear it from someone else first. There are books that help to explain sexuality to children. (See *Useful resources*.)

> You don't always know how much the children have been told. We don't think ours had been properly prepared. Shortly after they moved in, they asked if we were brothers. The social worker said she had explained but maybe they hadn't taken it on board or didn't really understand.
> *Max*

Dealing with your friends

Your friends may treat you differently after you have adopted children. Some may want to be more involved, whereas others may feel they have lost the carefree couple or friend they used to know. You may hope that friends will be more supportive than they turn out to be. You have to accept that it was your decision to adopt, not theirs. You may find that other parents you meet through your child's nursery or school become a new support network that you didn't have before. Parenting support programmes can help to overcome any feelings of isolation. (See *Useful resources*.)

> They want you to turn into this little golden family
> but in reality it's not like that. Some of our friends have
> backed off a bit. Some don't understand the intensity
> of it.
> *John*

Telling the children they are adopted

If you adopt a very young child, at some stage you will have to tell them that they are adopted. It is better to be up-front about this and make sure you are the first to tell the child, rather than he or she hearing it from someone else. There are quite a few books which help to explain adoption to a child. (See *Useful resources*.)

Most adoption agencies put together a life story book for the children with as much information about their early life and their birth family as possible, for them to refer to in later life. At the age of 18 in England, Wales and Northern Ireland and 16 in Scotland, adopted children have the right to their original birth certificate and can trace their birth families if there has been no previous contact.

Physical difficulties

A child who has been neglected or abused may have physical problems such as bed wetting or soiling or be more susceptible to certain conditions, for example, eczema. These may improve over time when the child settles in but if it persists, consult your doctor. The child may also need therapy to deal with past abuse or neglect.

Developmental difficulties

Children who have had a traumatic start in life may also develop more slowly than their peers. This may include not talking or walking as early, having a limited attention span, delayed motor skills or immature behaviour. They may not have been taught some skills such as using a toilet, eating properly or tying shoelaces. You will need to be very patient and accepting of developmental delays caused by neglect. A child may also have inherited problems from their parents, particularly if they abused alcohol or drugs. These may not manifest themselves until later life.

Emotional difficulties

A child who is adopted may have problems such as attachment disorder, where they find it hard to form trusting and secure relationships. They may also have low self-esteem, be overly aggressive or attention-seeking. They may have post-traumatic stress disorder and suffer recurrent memories of a traumatic past. You need to be alert to this possibility and seek medical and psychological help.

> They need to be reassured that things aren't going to keep going wrong in their lives, they might lack security, they might not understand what has happened to them, they might blame themselves.
> *Simon*

> I've thought a lot about the impact of the neglect on a child, for example, if they were just sat in a chair with no interaction in the first year of life. What psychological impact will this have long-term and can this be fixed? Will all the love in the world make up for what they might not have had in the first year?
> *Chas*

> I think some adopted children can be attention-seeking, quite bold and brassy with a kind of brittle toughness and a soft underneath. If you are a birth child, you

know where you come from and you never question
it – things are more certain. But with adopted children,
they know from a very young age that adults can be
unreliable. It can take time for them to build up trust.
Max

Not feeling an instant bond

You may have difficulty feeling an instant bond with your child.
Parents who have given birth sometimes report this, so don't expect
it to happen as soon as the child moves in. You may have feelings
of guilt or depression because you don't feel as happy as you had
expected in the build up to the adoption. You will probably question
if you have made the right choice but this is natural during a period
of massive change and adjustment. Make sure you read as much as
you can of other people's experiences and get as much support as
you can. (See Part II of this book and *Useful resources*.)

Some people have said it happens straight away and
others have said it can take three months. I think my
partner felt it from day one whereas I think it has
taken me longer – about two months. Until then I was
just getting on with it, doing the shopping, sorting out
arguments and then I suddenly thought I'd be really
sad if they weren't here tomorrow. It would be a
massive loss.
John

Adoption breakdown

It is a sad reality that some adoptions don't work out. The first three
months can be particularly stressful. If you see signs that all is not
well and there is a real danger of disintegration, talk to the adoption
agency and seek support. If a placement breaks down before an
adoption order is made, the adoption agency will still have parental

responsibility for the child and can remove the child. If the placement breaks down after the adoption order has been made, you will have sole parental responsibility and will have to place the child into the care of the local authority. You may be able to try again with another child, but the adoption panel and the adoption agency will have to consider whether to approve you again.

To find out about how other gay men and lesbians have dealt with some of these issues and to share some of their joy, read the case studies in the next section. Get your tissues at the ready!

PART TWO

Introduction

This section of the book focuses on the real-life experiences of gay men and lesbians who are at various stages of the adoption process. Some have recently been approved by the panel and are at the matching stage. Others are in the settling-in period with children recently having joined the family, while others adopted children several years ago.

There is a wide range of experiences from adopting sibling groups, to adopting children with special needs, through to adopting children from abroad and even one case where two lesbians have adopted a child with a different ethnic origin. The stories are told with compassion and honesty, detailing some of the difficulties children and parents have faced as well as the happiness and joy.

Names have been changed to protect identities.

6

Raymond and Pete

Raymond and Pete have been approved to adopt two children of either sex between the ages of three and nine. They are looking for a suitable match. Raymond, 44, and his partner Pete, 30, have lived together for nine years. They have always wanted to have a family but until the recent legal changes didn't think it was possible.

Why did you decide to adopt?

Raymond was adopted and would like to give something back, to offer a child a home. We didn't want to consider other ways of having children, such as surrogacy, as we felt there were too many emotional and financial risks involved.

What experience did you have of children beforehand?

Our experience of child care was fairly limited but when Raymond's sister gave birth, we became very involved, looking after his nephew twice a week, while his sister worked on night shifts. This was quite an eye-opening experience and was a good test for us.

What was the initial reaction of the adoption agencies?

Initially we did some research on the internet and decided to talk to an adoption charity. We had a ninety-minute meeting with them, where they explained what was involved and the timescales, which was very useful.

A week later they sent out an information pack with what seemed like a job description for being an adoptive parent. We felt that they were looking for perfection and this put us off. It felt like applying to do an NVQ in parenting, having to meet performance criteria and give evidence of prior learning or acquire new skills.

We then approached our local authority. However, it proved to be extremely bureaucratic and inefficient. In fact, we were rejected at the initial application stage because we were both smokers. We'd joined a smoking cessation class and were in the process of quitting but they didn't take that into account. We found their letter very patronising. It basically said don't bother trying anywhere else because nobody will touch you.

We then applied to a voluntary adoption agency in London but encountered a series of administrative problems, with a meeting being cancelled at short notice and then being given the wrong address for a second meeting. They had also told us that we would probably have to wait a long time, being white parents.

In the end, we went back to the adoption charity. Now, having gone through the selection process with them and looking back on the literature, the job specification is quite realistic. Perhaps it was designed to put some people off. Actually, they were being as transparent as possible.

What was your experience of the preparation course?

The five-day preparation course took place over three weeks. We enjoyed this, it was a good pace and I'm glad it was spread out. This made it manageable. It was very informative and gave us a lot to think about.

I found the examples of children the social workers talked about depressing. I appreciate that they give you worst-case scenarios but it did seem very bleak at times. I shared this with the group and other people agreed with me. You need something positive as well to know that it is all worthwhile.

How did you decide on your preference, e.g. adopting siblings, ages or sex of children?

We did more research after the course about child development so we would know what to expect at different stages. We also boned up on learning disabilities and what impact this could have on a child's life. After the preparation course, we had to fill in a form expressing preferences for a child, such as levels of disability. In all, there was a checklist of 50 points to consider, and we had to answer "yes", "no" or "would need more information" as answers. This was the hardest part for us.

We photocopied the form and filled it in separately. We then cross-referred and discussed any discrepancies. This helped us to clarify what we could deal with. We agreed that if one of us was unsure about a criterion then that was a no, otherwise it wouldn't work.

In the end, we gave a positive tick to six criteria, a negative to two and the rest, we said we would need more information, depending on the child's circumstances. We said we couldn't adopt a child with severe physical disabilities. We haven't got any scope to adapt our home as it is mid-terrace and there is a very small front and back garden.

What was your experience of the home study?

We enjoyed the home study. It was good to talk about our plans for the future and to reflect on the past. You quite often forget the good things that have happened in the past but I remembered friendships I formed as a child and how I used to play. It helped me to get into the framework of looking at things from a child's perspective.

We had five meetings with our social worker. Each meeting lasted three to four hours. I thought it was going to be very intrusive but it wasn't. I can understand if you've had really bad experiences that you could fear looking back at the past, but the social workers think that you need to look at all your experiences as they may help you identify with the difficult experiences a child has had.

What was your experience of the adoption panel?

The panel stage went well. The social worker had explained the process fully and we met the Chair and social worker before meeting the panel. They told us the questions we would be asked, so we had a few minutes to prepare our answers. I was a bit worried to start with, thinking should I say what they want to hear, but in the end it's best to be honest. I wanted them to approve us for who we are.

My advice to anyone going through the process is to be yourself. This way, any judgements made will be accurate and that is better for matching purposes. Don't skirt around issues.

What has been your experience of finding a match?

We haven't encountered any homophobia so far in the process, however, that might change now that we are looking for a match. Other social workers across the country will be judging our suitability and they can always reject us on the grounds of our sexuality but give another reason.

The matching stage is proving much more emotional. Until now we were in a bubble with our support group and social worker and everything was fairly straightforward. Now we've moved from if to when.

We are on the Adoption Register and can apply to other local authorities. We are also looking through *Be My Parent* magazine and *Children Who Wait*, Adoption UK 's family-finding magazine.

However, I find it frustrating having to wait to get information about children. Sometimes this takes several months to arrive. Often the Child's Permanence Reports (CPRs) have very little relevant information and some of it is a year out of date. We went through one CPR and found 20 areas where we needed more information. When the social worker supplied this, the history was more negative than the form had led us to believe. If social workers could provide relevant, up-to-date information, we could make the decision more quickly. The whole process would speed up and fewer children would languish in care.

The accuracy, standard of English and layout of the forms also varies enormously. One CPR was 150 pages long, while another was 20. On one form, two-thirds of the information was about the birth family. I also think it is a shame that information can't be emailed rather than posted.

It is a learning process, we are working out how to filter the information more efficiently. It is hard to reject children but you have to be realistic – you have to weigh up what the child needs and what you can offer.

One of the big problems I can foresee is agreeing the amount of contact with the birth family. Lots of people had issues with this on the preparation course. I don't think it allows the child to move on. Other adoptive parents have said it causes a lot of problems and is very unsettling for the child. I didn't know anything about my birth family until five years ago. We met up but it soon broke down and I think what happened to me in terms of being adopted was for the best. I think social workers should rethink the theories on contact with birth parents.

7

Rachel and Des

Rachel and Des, a white couple, have been together for ten years. They met in London, although Rachel is originally from New Zealand. Rachel is a solicitor and Des is a nurse. They have adopted a 22-month-old boy, who is of mixed ethnicity. Since the adoption, they have moved back to New Zealand. Rachel tells their story.

Why did you decide to adopt?

I always wanted to have children by both adopting and bearing them myself. My partner also wanted to start a family but did not want to be pregnant herself. Unfortunately, as it turned out, I have fertility issues. We looked at fertility treatment but decided to go with adoption instead.

What experience did you have of children beforehand?

We both had quite a bit of experience, Des having taken on a maternal role in caring for a much younger brother and me having a large extended family. More recent experience was mainly as godparents to two young girls who we'd look after overnight and take on day trips.

How did you decide on the adoption agency you chose?

We visited our local authority in London but got the impression that they were under-resourced and not particularly receptive. This may have been because we were a white couple when they needed more African-Caribbean and African adopters, rather than because we are gay.

We visited a voluntary agency, and were impressed by their professionalism, their reach (nationwide) and their positive response to us as gay adopters. We decided to go with the voluntary agency, as we felt comfortable with them.

What was your experience of the preparation course?

Positive – it was helpful doing it in a group environment where there were a number of different types of adopters. It was challenging and had us questioning ourselves whether we really wanted to do it – the answer was always a resounding yes.

How did you decide on your preference, e.g. adopting siblings, and ages and sex of children?

When we described the attributes of the child we hoped for, they tended to be traits more commonly associated with a boy rather than a girl. We did not, however, specify a gender preference, nor did we specify that we'd prefer one child over a sibling group – it all very much depended on the profiles of the children.

We wanted to be in a position to influence a child's life positively and to help them become a fully functioning adult – that set some parameters in terms of the children we'd consider. For instance, we would consider a child with learning difficulties depending on their severity and a child with a physical disability, again depending on the severity.

What was your experience of the home study?

Long, invasive, manipulative, educational and challenging! Our social worker knew exactly how to wind us up and get a reaction, particularly from me. We'd leave each session asking ourselves what was that about, what was the social worker trying to ascertain on that one?

What was your experience of the adoption panel?

Very welcoming and positive. We were well prepared, as were the panel and they asked relevant questions and made positive comments about what we could offer a child. The Chair, in particular, was very good at quelling any nerves. There was an awareness and respect for how much it meant to us and how much it would mean for the children.

What advice would you give to anyone going through these stages?

Don't put your life on hold for it.

What was your experience of finding a match?

This was mixed and overall it took about 18 months from approval to being matched. We studied *Children Who Wait* and *Be My Parent* every month and discussed any possible children with our social worker. Our social worker would then make contact with the child's social worker. Our social worker, who worked part-time, did a lot of legwork for us. We did, however, make some approaches, particularly if we saw a child advertised on the adoption websites. We also had to press to get our details put on the National Adoption Register.

At first we were linked with a girl, aged two, very quickly and we were visited twice by her social workers. The first visit went well and we thought that, subject to getting more information on the medical front and her legal status changing to having a placement order (under the new system), all seemed hopeful. The child's social worker then changed and the new one decided to come to London on a jolly just to check us out – he arrived late and left early, on a Friday afternoon. There didn't appear to have been any handover to him and he didn't ask any questions of significance, nor did he share with us the information that we'd asked for. Despite being linked with her, we decided to walk away a few months later because of the local authority's incompetence and lack of professionalism. About 12 months later, we saw the girl in Adoption UK 's family-finding magazine, *Children Who Wait*, still waiting for a home and with the same legal status. They very much let her down.

Our second link was with a two-year old boy. He was of dual heritage, white British and African-Caribbean. Our first visit from the social workers went very well. They told us there and then that they were going to recommend us and asked us to confirm availability for dates for panel. The social worker's boss wanted to meet us so they came out again, and again it went well. Unfortunately, news then came back that we were not "black enough" – information that was readily available on our profile and readily apparent on visiting us – it should not have taken two visits to determine this.

We do, however, live in a predominantly black area and our network is diverse.

Our third link was with a boy, aged 22 months when placed, with Black South African and Moroccan parentage. He was a relinquished child and had been with the same foster carer since birth. He was born in a very white, rural area of the UK and they had problems finding suitable adopters, so they looked to our adoption agency and to us. From first learning of him, things moved quickly, smoothly and professionally. The social services where he lived were brilliant.

What is your child like?

Our son came to live with us at age 22 months. He is a big lad, healthy and fun. His birth mother discovered late in her pregnancy that she was expecting and wasn't in a position to offer him all that she wanted for him. He was placed into foster care hours after the birth and had the same foster carer until we were matched.

I think the fact that he was born in a rather white part of the country was one factor as to why he wasn't matched sooner – this of course worked in our favour. Once the family finder extended the search beyond families with a close ethnic match, we were quickly their preferred option.

He'd had a couple of links before us with black families. We were told that they had considered him either "too black" or "not black enough" for their family. Their loss is very much our gain.

What was your experience of first meeting your son?

Wonderful. We went with the foster carer and collected him from nursery. He'd been shown our photo book and DVD in advance and the foster carer, a woman in her 60s, had prepared him well for his two mummies. On that first meeting, we left the nursery and he took my hand and we've not looked back.

What was it like in the first stages of settling in as a family?

Great. He settled in very well, although we did keep things simple and quiet to start with.

What emotional and behavioural issues have you dealt with?

I'd say he has been a typical toddler – entirely age-appropriate. We've been very lucky.

Have you had any contact with birth parents and family?

There hasn't been any although we would be open to it.

What has been your experience of dealing with the following?

School

Our son isn't at school but as part of preparation in anticipation of adoption (before we had a match) we visited and contacted local schools (both fee-paying and local authority schools). They were all very helpful, but the most helpful were the fee-paying schools – they could answer our questions most fully around such things as lessons where family issues might be discussed.

Friends and family

Our friends and family have largely been supportive. My partner's mother needed careful treatment but for some reason much preferred us to adopt than to give birth! My father similarly preferred us to become parents this way too. Both sets of parents have asked questions around role models, in particular male role models.

Discussing your sexuality with the children

Not an issue – we're very open and he's at an age where he hasn't quite started to challenge the differences in his family compared to others. We still talk to him about different families so as to lay the foundations for when or if it becomes an issue.

Ethnicity

We speak with him about our respective races and ethnicities. It hasn't been an issue for us as a family but when we looked to see whether there was any post-adoption support in our area, offered by our local authority, we were told in no uncertain terms that they did not support transracial adoptions. With that kind of rhetoric, we weren't going to be asking them for anything.

The foster family

Given the circumstances, our son had a very solid start in life. We do some things differently from the foster carer. For example, we're big on reading to children but she dismissed that as something he was not into. Yet with us we started reading from day one and haven't stopped. The foster carer prepared him well and admitted that, at first, she had reservations about same-sex adopters but after reading our profiles and meeting us she felt we'd be a wonderful family for him. She was very positive and supportive.

We did have concerns that she was finding it hard to let go – we had a number of phone calls after placement so we asked our son's social worker to make sure she was getting support.

Making a photo album/video

This was fun and not nearly as hard to do as we'd feared.

Playing one parent off against another

Our son does this – but we're alive to it and try to play it down and support each other. It's usually me on the wrong end of his wrath. Des and I talk things through and agree a course of action. It's so much easier to deal with when you have a plan and you can understand the psychology behind why he's doing it.

Leave from work, employers' and colleagues' attitudes

Both places of work were very supportive and except for one colleague of mine and one colleague of Des's (both rather religious), our colleagues have been great. We were also both allowed time off during the preparatory and home study stages to attend meetings. Des works for the NHS and she was entitled to adoption leave broadly comparable to the same package they offered for maternity leave. My employer had never dealt with adoption or a gay employee becoming a parent. They prepared a policy for adoption leave. I took the equivalent of paternity leave and extra time as annual leave.

Dealing with anger

If our son gets angry, we talk to him about it. It's okay to be upset, we all get angry sometimes. Even when the anger is directed at us, usually me, we try to remain calm and to reassure him that everything is okay. If we get upset, it only escalates the problem. We have a great book, *No Matter What*, which is fantastic at reiterating to a child that, no matter what, you'll still love him.

What effect has it had on your own relationship?

Our relationship is stronger, although our sex life has suffered. We need to find ways to spend more time together alone.

What does your son call you?

Mummy Rachel or Rachel, Mummy Des or Desy.

How do you deal with misunderstandings?

We deal with it head on. I say, 'I *am* his mother' – usually in response to 'Oh, isn't his mother collecting him today?' When challenged, we clarify and say he has two mothers, we are both his parents.

8

John and Dan

John and Dan, who are both white, adopted two boys aged six and seven, who are also both white. John, 45, was adopted himself, in the sixties. He has a well-paid job in retail and took paternity leave when the boys moved in. Dan is 35.

Why did you decide to adopt?

From my perspective, adoption has always been part of my life, so I always thought I could adopt. Whereas my partner, Dan, had shut his mind to the fact that he would ever be a parent – he puts it down to his Catholic upbringing.

We first started talking about it seven or eight years ago but Dan wasn't keen, he said he didn't want to be a dad. Then we had a conversation about four years ago when he got really emotional and said he did want to be a father. We finally decided to go ahead with it in January 2006 when the law changed so we could both legally be adoptive parents. This was important to Dan. I think all the other stuff about civil partnerships also helped.

We did think about having a birth child. We know five lesbian couples who have had babies. Some have a fantastic relationship with the father and he is a part of their life but others have said you've donated sperm and that is it, or you come when we say but don't try to be a parent.

We did think about this with two friends of friends but we weren't comfortable with what they were asking. They didn't want our name on the birth certificate, they didn't want us to ever take the child on holiday or for the child to stay the night. It made us realise we wanted to be full-time parents.

What was the initial reaction of the adoption agency/ies?

In January 2006, we had our first meeting with our social worker. She had never dealt with a same-sex male couple. She was really good. She said 'I apologise if I say anything inappropriate and please tell me if I do'. She told us there and then that we could go forward to the next stage, which is the preparation course.

It was really strange, we were driving up the hill on the first day and we suddenly thought, shit, what are we doing, we might be the only same-sex couple there, people might not want us there.

Until this point, we had felt like we were in the middle of the process, like a project, you take it step-by-step, whereas other people are getting really excited or concerned for you. Other people thought it was massive, which we kind of knew but we weren't thinking of it every day.

What was your experience of the preparation course?

There were 12 of us. There was a couple from Nigeria, who never voiced it but you got the impression that they would have preferred us not to be there but they never said anything and they were fine with us.

I'd said to Dan I didn't want to make an issue of being adopted and that I wasn't going to tell them, although obviously the social worker knew. However, they said on day one, honesty is absolutely paramount. I was shocked when people on the course were saying stuff like it wouldn't be a big issue to change a child's name and questioning why they couldn't travel with children as soon as they had them. Or that they wanted a playmate for their other child. I was dumbfounded.

I said to Dan quietly, 'I am going to have to tell them I'm adopted because this is crazy'. At the end of the course people said it was really useful to have my opinion as an adopted person.

I've always worked in teams and you know when to speak, when to be quiet, when to challenge. There were definitely some people who were struggling more on the course because they weren't used to having to interact in groups and share stuff.

One of the social workers who was facilitating it was fantastic. She said at the end, 'We don't normally do this but I'd really like to be your case study social worker'. We thought she was great.

What was your experience of the home study?

The home visits started three weeks after the course finished in May and we were approved in November that year. Some other friends who were adopting at the same time needed eight joint referees and four individual ones each. We only needed four referees. I know a lot of people have been given a hard time about how much childcare experience they have had and have been sent away to get more. They accepted that we had close relationships with nieces and nephews. We also have a lot of straight friends with children. I'm still really good friends with my previous partner's sister and her children and have seen them grow up.

Some parts of the home study were really hard. We had to prepare a time line and she wanted a short sentence about a significant thing you could remember in every year. I could remember my brother being born when I was two-and-a-half. To pick up stuff from all those years was hard, like when you split up from your previous partner or when people had died. There were happy things as well, but seeing it all listed on a piece of paper was really difficult. I started to get angry about things I hadn't thought of in a long time.

Some of it is really relentless, like they would ask about your parenting style with examples such as if you came home and found your son or daughter in bed with another man or woman, what would you do? If they went out for the night and refused to come home, what would you do?

In the end, we both said we can't tell you in exactly every situation what we would do, we would just hope the way we bring them up would minimise those situations and that we would deal with them appropriately because we have built up a good relationship with the children.

The social worker also saw us both separately. There were some surprises. I thought I would be more authoritarian than my partner but he is more authoritarian than me. It brought up some interesting stuff in our relationship because it is stuff you wouldn't normally talk about.

Through all of this, we didn't think there was any homophobia until right at the end, we had to meet the social worker's line manager just before we went to panel and that was really uncomfortable. She kept saying 'people like you' and there were big pauses.

It's difficult because you don't want to rock the boat or complain because you think they will shove you to the back of the queue or say no. When we went to panel, they only asked us four or five questions. We were in there for 25 minutes. They did ask about our lifestyle. We said we'd still be able to go out to dinner or go on holiday. I think afterwards they might have meant going clubbing and stuff.

We really enjoyed the whole experience. It was tough and there were some challenges but we felt supported and it was positive.

What was your experience of finding a match?

Unfortunately, just after we were approved, our social worker went home to Australia so we had to have a new social worker. It became really hard because they weren't doing what they should have been doing. We had one who told us we should have as many children on the go at once, up to 15. Dan at the time was doing the research and had to balance all these case studies coming through and contacting social workers. It was getting really pressurised.

At one point, although they had said we couldn't adopt children from Eastern Europe unless we could prove a connection, they suddenly suggested we took two children that were half Tanzanian, half English, born as Muslims and being brought up as Catholics. You do panic because you think perhaps these are the only children we'll ever be offered.

Dan said we should go and see these children's social worker, but I said it was a recipe for disaster and not what we wanted. Their skin is a different colour to ours, so when we are walking down the street it will be obvious. It is not fair on them.

We also came very close to adopting two boys who were the youngest of 11 siblings. There had been sibling-on-sibling abuse in the family but they had managed to remove the two youngest boys before they had been abused. But the birth father, who had a penchant for young girls, kicked up such a fuss about us being a same-sex couple. We challenged this, pointing out that they were giving more credence to a man with a reputation for sleeping with under-age girls and who has a family with sibling-on-sibling abuse. We were absolutely furious.

There were another two children in a London borough but the authorities said they need a mummy and a daddy. Our social worker thought this was homophobic. We then had another social worker who was useless. She just disappeared and the council kept making excuses for her over three weeks.

At one point, Dan phoned me in tears and said, 'I can't do this any more'. In the end, I thought I don't care if I upset the council now, so I rang the head of department, whom we had met briefly, and told her what had been happening. She was absolutely horrified. She said you should never have more than two or three children on the go at once and that we shouldn't be making calls to the children's social workers. That is when they admitted that the two social workers we'd had previously were on temporary contracts. A couple of days later they got us one of our original social workers and things sped up after that.

Four social workers came from the north to see us twice, and on a practical level you are thinking they must be keen. But when we started to know more about the children, we knew it wasn't right for us and we had to say no. I know two people who said no twice during matching, which was really hard, really heartbreaking. You have to watch out for social workers glossing over details because they are desperate to place children.

You do have to be really proactive, get the newspaper, *Be My Parent*, sit down and circle the children you think you could adopt and then go back over and narrow it down to two. Then ring the editor of *Be My Parent*. If they think you might be suitable, they give you the child's social worker's details and then you phone them and register an interest. It is then supposed to be between the two social workers but you do have to keep phoning and sending out a mini CV, which is an overview of you as a couple with photographs and what you might be looking for. You have to send this out to as many local authorities as possible and make sure your social worker puts you on the National Adoption Register. Keep calling your own social worker to make sure it's all live and it's happening.

Be really clear about what you will and won't accept, for example, whether you can adopt children with disabilities, learning difficulties or those who have been sexually abused. You have to state your preferences and stick to that and remind yourself of what you want. For example, we said right from day one that we didn't want to take on children who had been sexually abused or had learning difficulties. That might be right for other people but it's not right for us. We always wanted two boys.

It was a tortuous process from August to April between the panel approval and matching. The first two meetings with the children's social worker were about a month apart. We then met the foster parents a month later and apparently the foster father wasn't sure it was a good idea for the children to go to a same-sex couple but he came round. We didn't meet the school staff and doctors until the January, so it was all drawn out. There were another two boys in the north of England whom we came quite close to adopting.

We also had to balance what we wanted, as originally we had asked for pre-school age children and we've ended up with a six- and seven-year-old. I was worried but my partner said, 'Are we going to throw all this away just because they are a year or two older?'

We met the boys' teachers in the January and they couldn't have been more positive about them. The headmistress was nearly in tears at the thought of losing them. We came away from that thinking thank God, that was a big breakthrough.

What was your experience of meeting the children?

The process was absolutely exhausting. We were living in a cottage near where the boys lived, during the introductions stage. You are totally reliant on the foster parents as it's their home. That first day when you are sitting on their sofa and they say, 'We'll go and get your children', is really surreal. And they come trotting round the corner. We had seen loads of photos and a DVD but to actually see them in the flesh was amazing.

The foster parents were great. They have a massive garden and they just backed off and left us with them and we took it at our own speed. After four days, they said it is going so well; take them out for a full day if you want to. Towards the end of the process, we were all exhausted and the children must have been as well; the younger child, Jack, started having big tantrums in the foster home when we left.

I think because of his life experiences, Jack has had to grow up quicker but in other ways he has missed out on a lot of other experiences. We had this mad two weeks when we did loads of stuff with them that they had never done before like going to the beach, the zoo and the cinema. They weren't used to having two people totally focused on them. It was like a massive holiday for them but at the same time they had to go back to the foster home where there were three other foster children. They were also attached to the foster mum, who had done a brilliant job. So Jack was saying he didn't want to leave her because he loved her.

It was not until the end that we actually saw one of his tantrums. He'd gone to bed while we were there and he just went mad, throwing his suitcases down the stairs and saying, 'I'm not leaving'. Since his birthday a few weeks ago, that intensity has gone. But when he had this tantrum, he was hitting the foster mother in the chest. He can use very adult language. He was saying, 'You are not taking me and you are not having my brother either, you're horrible, you're taking me away, this is your last chance to prove you want me, you don't really want me'. We would be saying, 'That's really sad, Jack, but we do want you to come and live with us'.

Don't underestimate how difficult it is on the day you take them from the foster parents' house. You get swept along in those introductions and everything is going well, and then suddenly we had to turn up at ten o'clock on a Wednesday morning. They'd had a big leaving do the night before, friends from school had come, and the sofa was full of presents. Everybody is standing around – the social worker, the foster carers – and you have to put them in the car. Jack had been fine up to that point, hadn't had a tantrum, and then suddenly he is upstairs in the house saying, 'You are making me move again...I'm losing my friends...I don't understand my life. This isn't fair, everybody just leaves me'. We were all crying.

Colin didn't have a tantrum, although he had been the one having tantrums before. He was very calm. It was the hardest thing to drive out of their drive with these boys. I was thinking, they've got a life, they've got friends, a school, and I should be moving there, not them moving to my borough. That is really hard. My partner said I was in tears in the car down the motorway and I didn't realise it.

In the first few weeks we didn't protect ourselves enough about saying what was right for us. At the first review, you see an independent social worker. She said, 'Why are you calling the foster parents every week? That is not right for you. Do it in two weeks' time, and then a month, and then every six months, and perhaps see them in the future on special occasions.'

To get Colin to understand that was really hard, but the last time we spoke to them, he said, 'We are now only seeing you on special occasions', and he explained it to them.

What was it like in the first stages of settling in as a family?

In the first three-and-a-half weeks, we really thought we'd made a mistake. Dan doesn't get stressed easily but he was picking up a heavy chair in our living room and dropping it in a rage to release his tension.

The social workers had warned us not to tell the boys that we like anything in particular. For example, Jack would say, 'You like my trainers, don't you?', and you'd say yes and the next minute he'd be trying to rip them up. Or he'd say, 'You love Papa and I'm going to stab him because you're not having him'.

He'd also threaten us, saying, 'I'm going to lie to social services about what you've done to me and they are going to believe me, not you'. He would also threaten to kill himself. He still does that. He tries to strangle himself or punch himself in the head, saying, 'You don't want me here, you don't love me, you're not my real daddy, and I want my mummy'. He uses the f-word and c-word a lot, with everything usually ending with snake or skunk.

We really did think this was too much. One day Dan couldn't breathe. I said, you are going to have to go out. It was so intense. It was strange that the older one, Colin, was trying to be the most perfect child. I think in his mind, he was thinking if Jack carries on like this then they are going to get rid of us, so I need to compensate. So he would say, 'Jack is ruining everything, stop him, stop him!'.

So there has been lots of holding Jack until he calms down. But you are only human and one day I did snap and said, 'OK, if you want to leave, there's my mobile phone. When you get up in the morning, that's fine, we'll call the social worker and we can end this now if you want to'. Then he sat there for ten minutes and said, 'I think I've really upset you, so the worst thing I could do to you is to stay, so I'm not going anywhere, I'm going to stay and ruin your life'.

What emotional and behavioural issues have you dealt with?

We've just had to be calm even when he's saying, 'I'm going to kill myself'. We've had to say, 'OK if that's what you want to do'. He wants you to make a big thing of it. Sometimes he'll say, 'That's it, I'm leaving, I'm going to find my mummy now'. You just have to say, 'OK, that's up to you'. We've had to not escalate it. Some days it is really hard. What we have been really keen to do is keep the same routines as the foster parents, so they always go to bed at 7.30. There's also the naughty chair with a timer on the oven clock and when that is up the child can get up again. We also count to three and if they haven't done what you are asking by three, they go on the chair; they usually do it by two.

I think sometimes people think, oh, they are adopted, we need to give them some leeway, whereas we have tried not to. I have seen other guys making that mistake, thinking, oh, he's had a horrible life.

With them being a bit older than we wanted, I think we have missed out a bit on some of the cute things they say when they are younger, but they are really intelligent children and top of their school years. This is amazing considering everything that has happened to them. They are great characters ninety-five per cent of the time.

Another thing that is hard about them being older is that they will start to talk about mummy and daddy. Jack left mummy when he was three so he doesn't have some of the bad memories that Colin has, so he thinks someone has taken his mummy away.

We went out the other night and he said, 'Mummy is still in Wales, isn't she?', and I know she isn't but social workers have told us not to tell them where she is. So Jack says, 'I'm going to find her when I'm 18'. Whereas Colin says, 'No way, I'm never going to see her again', because he remembers mummy drunk, on drugs, having other men in the house, daddy dying. He remembers all of that.

Jack has said some of the stuff he knows is because Colin or the social workers have told him. But he started to tell me last night about the day they were finally taken away and he said, 'Mummy went in an ambulance because she had been drinking too much'. It is really hard to listen to that sometimes and they really pick up on stuff. For example, I sighed and Jack said, 'You told us we could talk about mummy and daddy and now you are making that noise'. I said, 'you can, you can but I'm just a little bit tired today'.

Sometimes, when they are misbehaving, they are looking you in the eye and you think, you know exactly what you are doing, you know how to press the buttons. Jack went through this whole thing of chanting mummy, mummy constantly when he was cross. It is also hard when they are telling us stuff that they haven't told social services, for example, being tied into golf bags and the golf bags being hit or the time when they were locked into the bottom of the divan overnight or daddy getting them out of bed when he got home and hitting them.

We've got psychotherapy and counselling appointments for them individually and us as a family. Jack is easier to talk to sometimes; even at six years old, he'll say, 'Sad things have happened to me in my life and bad things and I know I'll never forget but if I talk about them, I will feel better and it will help me with the rest of my life'. Whereas Colin, because his memories are more real, asks why we have to keep talking about the sad things. He says, 'There are lots of nice things in my life, I don't want to talk about the sad things'. So you do have to push him a bit to talk about things.

Meanwhile, Jack, the younger one, has settled in and now Colin has gone the other way. He has big screaming fits. He doesn't get violent like Jack but gets hysterical about nothing. This morning he was laying on the floor having hysterics ten minutes before leaving for school, and he's saying, 'You know you want to hit me, you know you want to punch me, hit me now!. You start trying to be nice to him and he says, 'Stop it, I don't like it when you are nice to me, stop it, it scares me, be horrible!.

One of the children last night said, 'This is my real home, I love you', and then this morning said, 'You are worse than my birth father'. I burst into tears when they'd gone to school but you know he is doing it to wind you up.

I know that as a child he was locked into a washing machine for a few hours and all these terrible things happened to him, but at the same time, you don't want to say that's really awful, you can do what you want now, or he'll grow into a vile adult.

Have you had any contact with birth parents and family?

It is a very complicated family history, and there's another child, Jane, who is 11 now. The mother turned up drunk at a family friend's and left Jane when she was 18 months old and never took her back again. The family friend took Jane on as her own child but never told her that she wasn't her birth mother. Colin and Jack know about Jane but she doesn't know about them.

Now their mother has reappeared, which we haven't told the boys about, and my partner's parents have a holiday home really near where she is now living so we can't go there any more. The boys ask why we aren't going there any more. So there is all that history to deal with and wondering how that is going to affect them.

We have also had to be quite tough about reducing contact with the foster parents. Some people have said when you walk out the door, that's it. Others have become friends and with us they were supposed to have had weekly phone calls but Jack was using that as a threat. You have to be tough with them. Your initial feeling is that you don't want to upset them, but I have had to say, you can threaten me as much as you like, but what were your foster parents doing? They were doing a job and if you go back into care you won't go back to them, you'll go to another foster family. Then he'll say, 'What if you and Papa were really ill?' And I have to say, 'You would stay with someone in our family or you'd stay with a foster carer in this area. You wouldn't go back to the county you came from'. It sounds really horrible but you do have to say no.

From being adopted myself, I can relate to the fact that whatever mummy and daddy have done, whether they are violent or drug addicts, they still were mummy and daddy. As an adopted person, you can think I'm quite happy where I am, but you think, what would have happened if I'd stayed with the birth mum and dad?

I think when children want to find out about their birth family or see their adoption file, you shouldn't think that is because you haven't been good parents.

What are some of the other issues you have dealt with?

Friends and family

When we started to talk to friends about it everyone was really excited, although my mum and dad weren't happy to start with. Although they had always treated Dan in the same way as my sisters-in-law, in terms of birthday and Christmas money, they never said who he was until about two-and-a-half years ago.

I think for my mum it was seeing stuff in the newspapers about civil partnerships and adoption and realising that everyone else was really supportive of our lives as a couple. These things combined so that she finally sent us a Christmas card 'To my son and his partner'. I phoned her to say, 'Thank you, that means a lot', and she said, 'You deserve it, and what's for dinner on Boxing Day?'!

I told her about our deciding to adopt before the whole process started, and about two weeks later she phoned and asked, 'Have you done anything about it?' She tried to say I was too old, that I might not be strong enough, that it might bring up too many memories for me. Gradually, she came round to it.

My dad was in hospital about six months into the adoption process. When we left after visiting him, the wife of the man in the next bed asked my mum if I was gay, and they got into a discussion, as her son was also gay. She suddenly got into one-upmanship with this woman, asking where their sons were getting married, and she boasted that we were adopting! By the time we came to negotiating about the boys in August last year, my mum said she couldn't wait to have more grandchildren and she was totally supportive of the whole thing.

You also have to be understanding of other people in your life. My closest friend was petrified that she would lose me as a friend because I was having children. You have to reach out to other people, saying 'This is going to be alright, we'll still be friends'. She said that the first time we went out together after the boys arrived, she was relieved that I was the same. People are sometimes scared for you.

You need to ask your friends for help sometimes. We have a big circle of friends who have children and that has helped. We were advised not to introduce them to a lot of people straight away but within the first few weeks we were going a bit stir-crazy so we started to introduce them and it went well, it didn't feel like they were confused. We told the social worker and she said you just have to do what is right, and now they are on their second or third time of meeting people. Dan did a gallery of photos of friends and an extended family tree to explain who was who.

Work

My company offers the same conditions for adoption leave as they do for maternity leave. It is one of the best in the industry – 20 weeks on full salary. That was one of the reasons we could do it financially. The company has been really supportive, so that has also helped.

When I left work, I said I'd rather keep it low-key in case it breaks down or goes wrong. But of course as soon as they advertised my job for adoption leave, the whole office went mad. They gave me loads of vouchers, presents and cards. My boss gave a speech in tears.

I had really mixed feelings about leaving my job for six months and knowing I was going to meet my children the following Tuesday. The whole office wants it to be a great success and so do our friends. So when something goes wrong, like one of the children hits me or they want to leave, it's like you have to deal with other people's disappointment as well. They want you to turn into this little golden family but in reality it's not like that. Some of our friends have backed off a bit. Some don't understand the intensity of it.

We've gone from two of us for 13 years to four of us. It is a big change for the person who gives up work. I'm used to a reasonably pressurised and good job and suddenly I am looking after children. It's a lot to get your head around.

Attachment

There's also the issue of how quickly you get attached to them. Some people have said it happens straight away and others have said it can take three months. I think my partner felt it from day one whereas I think it has taken me longer – about two months. Until then I was just getting on with it, doing the shopping, sorting out arguments and then I suddenly thought, I'd be really sad if they weren't here tomorrow. It would be a massive loss.

We both got panicky at the beginning thinking that they are never going to be fully our children, they've got too many memories, and this isn't going to work. But after a few weeks, you think, they will feel like ours, who are they going to be with the longest?

When you get children who aren't babies, you are always going to have to deal with the fact they have memories. And most of the gay community are not going to get babies. A few guys have got toddlers but I don't know anyone who has a baby. We were the first male couple to be approved in our borough but they made it clear from day one that it was highly unlikely that we would get a baby.

Homophobia

In terms of homophobia, there are things you have to think about more, for example, we've been on holiday to Turkey for years but in a predominantly Muslim country, will we stick out like a sore thumb? I don't want to be paranoid but I also don't want the children to feel uncomfortable.

The boys' social worker said she had to challenge some homophobia in the department when people had said they shouldn't go to a same-sex couple. I know we have been lucky compared with some of the stories on websites. I think we took longer to be matched because we were a same-sex couple. It took between November and April for us to find a match.

Schools

The schools here have been great. The children couldn't both get into the same school to start with but they will do in September. There is one male same-sex couple and three female couples as parents already. It doesn't seem to have been an issue for the boys.

Before we met the boys, we did a photo album with pictures of every room and the cat, the car, everything. They got them the day before we met them and Colin took them straight into school. By the time we got to the school, we were like mini celebrities, people were saying, 'Oh, you are the boys' dads'. So that was all really positive.

Your relationship

I think you have to really question your relationship with your partner because it is enormously stressful. Sometimes you don't realise how stressful it is but you need to take time out for yourself as well, and if something doesn't feel right you have to have the strength to say no, like we did with those Tanzanian children.

Do you have any other advice?

You have to be clear about what you want and be clear about the timescales. We set ourselves a limit, we had put our lives on hold since January 2006 and we wouldn't do it beyond August 2008. We had a good life beforehand and although it would be sad if it didn't work out, we could pick up our life and carry on.

Finding schools took a long time, going through all the Ofsted reports. Even buying a car seat took ages trawling through the internet.

Now with the boys, things take much longer to do, like going to the bank or post office takes twice as long. You have to give yourself space as well. My partner works most Saturdays but I had to say, it's great to do stuff as a family when you are off but I also need to go out and do something by myself. I can't be here all the time or it does my head in a bit.

You have to be strong. I think social services expect you to die on the altar of adoption. For example, I had always been really clear about taking six months off and possibly one more after that, but otherwise we can't afford it. Suddenly, in January, they said that these boys have had so many changes in their lives, it's not appropriate that you go back to work after six–seven months. We think you should go part-time. But I said, 'We have always been clear about this and if it's going to be a deal breaker then we are going to have to stop'. I felt it was very inappropriate and unfair to throw that in at a late stage. Then they backed off, so you have to set your boundaries. It would be really easy to say yes to whatever social services demands of you, but I think it's a really big mistake.

I've got other friends who are adopted and there are so many similarities between us. For example, in times of crisis, instead of inviting people to help you, you think, I'm much better at dealing with this on my own because I've only got myself to rely on. And I can already see Colin doing that sometimes. One day recently, he came out of school in a really bad mood and anything I said or did, he said he could deal with it without me. And I could tell what he was doing. It is very much on his terms how friendly he is or how close he lets people get to him.

It is difficult to hear them talk about the bad things that have happened to them, but you have to allow them space to do that.

Know your boundaries and make sure you give yourself space, otherwise you'll agree to things you don't want to agree to.

It is definitely really worthwhile doing this, and we do feel like a family now, but it's a lot of work to get there. It is so different from the sixties – my adoption file is an inch thick, but the boys have a large suitcase stuffed full of DVDs, reports, photographs, etc. It was more about the adult wanting a child then; quite rightly, it is the other way round now.

Another thing to watch out for is the children wanting to reject us before we reject them. That is what a lot of their behaviour is about. We find if one child becomes the devil-child, the other becomes the angelic child. Don't beat yourself up too much. Sometimes I wish I hadn't said things but you are only human. They will stir up an amazing amount of emotion in you. You can't be the perfect parent. I just sound like my mum the whole time! You need to be able to be honest with your partner and talk about what's gone on in the day when the children have gone to bed.

9

Chas and Simon

Chas and Simon, who are both white and in their thirties, have been approved to adopt two siblings of either sex aged six and under, and are waiting to be matched. They used to run their own company but sold it to concentrate on other interests, including becoming parents. They tell their story.

Why did you decide to adopt?

Chas: About five years ago I started talking about it, thinking it would be nice to have a family. We were thinking about adoption and looked at a website that had details of some children who were looking for adopters. They had severe disabilities and this made us think about it a lot more seriously and we realised we weren't ready for that at that time. We were running a business together and there was no guarantee it would survive. We didn't have much stability and didn't feel we could take on the responsibility of children.

Simon: Two years ago, we got married and sold the business. We then took stock of life and although we had some interesting projects, I felt there was something substantial missing. I wanted something more meaningful, so I brought up the idea of adopting again.

Chas: I wasn't so sure as we had only just finished working on the business, but when I started to realise how long it could take, we started to investigate it.

What was the initial reaction of the adoption agency?

Simon: We went to see our local authority for an initial chat. That was really helpful as they were very supportive of same-sex adoption and had placed children with same-sex adopters before. They said it was good to think about it for six months and get some more childcare experience, go on Adoption UK's message board and join BAAF.

Chas: I think I was still worried about a child not having a mother but they reassured us that we could be like a mother. They said there were so many things we could give to a child without actually being a mother. They really bolstered our confidence.

How did you get more experience of child care?

Simon: I found a local charity that goes into primary schools and teaches children about environmental issues. I went in and led paper-making sessions with five-year-olds. That was really good and gave me confidence. I also trained to be an independent visitor. This is a role that adoption charities and other adoption agencies have. It is an adult who has regular contact with a child in care. It is voluntary and you are there to be a friend who is consistent, like a mentor. The training was useful but I didn't go through with it as they hadn't come up with a match and it was getting close to the time when we might adopt.

The best experience we had was looking after two friends' children. They have a one-year-old and a three-year-old and we took care of the children one day a week for six months. We went over to their house just before breakfast and took over the child care until just before bedtime. We took them to nursery, changed nappies, and all that kind of stuff.

Chas: We got to know how we worked together as parents and our strengths and weaknesses and watched how the children developed.

How did you decide on a local authority?

Simon: We eventually went to a different local authority to the one we live in because we wanted to increase our chances of adopting. Sometimes local authorities want to find adoptive parents outside their area so the birth family doesn't live too near. There were also only three London boroughs that were taking on white adopters as they already had enough on their books and they mainly have black, minority ethnic or mixed-race children to place.

Chas: The local authority we went for were very supportive at the initial interview. They told us within a week that they wanted to take us on but that there could be a six-month delay before they could assign a social worker. In fact it was only two months.

Simon: Unfortunately, they weren't running a preparation course for six months. So we ended up having five home visits before the preparation course and then the social worker asked us the same questions after the preparation course in more depth so it felt as if it dragged on. It will have been 15 months between the first meeting and the panel. However, it has been good to have some thinking time and read about adoption.

Chas: I asked directly whether the type of children they place with gay and lesbian adopters are different from the type they place with straight adopters and they said no. I'm interested to know if there is generally discrimination against gay and lesbian adopters, in terms of us getting "harder to place" children.

Simon: It helps that our own social worker is an advocate for us but there are more people involved in the placement. For example, the child's social worker might be prejudiced.

Chas: It would be good to know the time lag between approval and matching for gay and lesbian adopters compared with heterosexual adopters. However, it is difficult to get a base line as it might be shorter if gay and lesbian adopters are more willing to adopt "harder to place" children.

Simon: There could also be a self-fulfilling prophecy, if gay men and lesbians think they are more likely to get a placement if they opt for "harder to place" children.

Chas: It would also be good to get some research on the outcomes of gay and lesbian adoptions. However, this could also be tricky if gay and lesbian adopters have taken on "harder to place" children, as there might be more breakdowns or more issues in later life.

Simon: You need some way of measuring added value, like they do with schools' performance and taking into account what you start with.

How did you find the preparation course?

Simon: It was good – just us and two other couples. You feel drained at the end of the day, talking about emotional subjects and opening up to strangers. Most of it was about making sure we understood what the different issues are likely to be.

Chas: They ask you how you would cope in different scenarios, for example, if a child is angry or withdrawn. They also expect you to have read quite a lot about issues such as attachment disorders, autism or attention deficit disorder.

Simon: They are trying to find adopters who will be good for specific problems children might have. They want to find out your strengths and weaknesses and match your strengths to the children's needs, for example, if you are good at drawing people out who might be shy or coping calmly when children are angry.

Chas: It is a strange mix between them teaching you about adoption and the type of children you might adopt. At the same time, they are also assessing you, your childhood and your background and your thoughts.

How did you decide on your preferences, for example, adopting siblings, and the ages and sex of children?

Simon: We have a preference for two siblings.

Chas: Initially we said one child and as young as possible and then as we have gone through the process, we have thought older is OK. There aren't that many younger children waiting for adoption.

Simon: In fact, the local authority said they might not have taken us on if we hadn't been prepared to take on two children.

Chas: As the process has gone on, we have realised there are definite advantages to taking on two, as we have always wanted two children anyway.

Simon: By adopting two at once, we can throw all our energies into it.

Chas: We don't need to go through the adoption process twice and also risk upsetting the first child.

Simon: We are expecting it to be hard work taking on two but it's sensible given our circumstances.

Chas: The more it has gone on, the less rigid we have become about their ages as well. We are now saying up to six whereas two years ago we would have said under four.

Simon: It has helped getting to know other adopters and seeing the pros and cons of different age groups and adopting siblings or one child. In the end they are all really nice kids. Even at six, it's not as if they've grown up, they are still very young.

Chas: The other thing about adopting older children is that you know if there are any medical issues or development issues. A lot of the issues that affect children in care will be evident, whereas if they are a year old, you might not know.

Simon: There are fewer unknowns, less uncertainties with the older children.

Chas: You know a bit more what you will be dealing with. However, there are so many issues with children in care.

Simon: You could drive yourself mad trying to decide what you can deal with but it is only when you look at the details of a particular child that you can really think about whether that is right for you.

And what about the sex of the child?

Chas: Ideally, we would like a boy and a girl.

Simon: If they were both the same, I'd rather it was two boys. I feel more confident with boys than girls generally.

Chas: The social worker said it was important to say what you do and don't want. The last thing they want is for you to take on children whom you are not comfortable with and for it not to work out. They want you to be as open and honest as possible.

And how have you found the home study?

Simon: It's been good apart from two sessions after the preparation course, when we felt the social worker didn't understand where we were coming from. I think it's important to have a good relationship with the social worker.

Chas: The home study has been more about getting to know us really well so she can match us.

Simon: There is a lot of discussion on the message boards about how much you should prepare your home. You could argue that everything should be tidy but then they might think you won't cope with children because your house is too spic and span because it will be turned upside down when children arrive!

Chas: At some point they will come round to the house and do a health and safety check.

Simon: They already told us we had to put banisters in, which we've done. And we'll need to put catches on the cupboards and make sure electrical items are safe. Apparently, they are also supposed to pay a surprise visit.

Chas: One time our social worker came an hour early, I don't know if that was the surprise visit for us. It was a bit strange.

What advice would you give to people going through the stages before going to panel?

Simon: Be patient, do as much research and reading as you can.

Chas: *A Child's Journey through Placement*, by Vera Fahlberg, was good. It is quite detailed and aimed at social workers but it goes into the psychology and facts about children in care.

Simon: The message boards were really helpful. You can ask questions and get answers really quickly. We have also met up with same-sex adopters and their children through a support group called New Family Social. It has been very reinforcing to see gay parents in action. You can read as much as you like but just seeing two mums or two dads doing normal things with children and being very natural – that was very encouraging.

Getting childcare experience was really useful. That made us feel more confident.

Chas: I think it's also important to talk to family and friends so that they understand what you are going through, as you'll need their support once it all happens.

Simon: Once you get started, you realise just how much there is to know about adoption.

Chas: A lot of people have a simplistic view that there are children out there waiting to be adopted and they will be grateful for their new home but that isn't necessarily the case.

Simon: They need to be reassured that things aren't going to keep going wrong in their lives, they might lack security, they might not understand what has happened to them, they might blame themselves.

Chas: It will be very quick once a match is found – you meet the foster carer, teacher, the GP and social worker. We also see some photos of the children and some of their history but often there isn't much, for example, there might not be any information about the birth father.

Simon: You don't actually meet the child until the placement has been approved. It will be such an intense moment, meeting a child or children for the first time and thinking they are your children. What do you say? What do you first talk about when you first meet your children? I've had dreams about this of a child coming up the drive and that is the first time I've met them.

In reality, we will meet them in the foster home initially over a week or so. The first day you meet them for an hour, the next day you take them to the park, and you work up to them coming to your house.

Chas: Hopefully, the child will have been well prepared. You make a story book about your life with pictures of the house and the cats and information about us. They see that before they meet you. We have thought about making a video as well.

What are some of your final thoughts at this stage?

Chas: I've thought a lot about the impact of neglect on a child, for example, if they were just sat in a chair with no interaction in the first year of its life. What psychological impact will this have long-term and can this be fixed? Will all the love in the world make up for what they might not have had in the first year?

Simon: I think it's a common misconception that once you adopt, the child will be yours and they will be fine.

Chas: You need to be realistic about development issues that arise for children taken into care and that you might not be able to fix it. You will probably succeed in lots of ways but there might be something that you can never correct.

Simon: It can be shocking reading about the previous life of your child but it is also very important to understand what their behaviours mean. They probably won't be able to tell you why they are behaving in a certain way. You need to understand why they are doing these things and what to do to try to help them. Mind you, it's hard to keep everything in your head, you just have to take each thing as it comes and go back to the books or social workers for advice if you need it.

Chas: Parenting is hard full stop. Nobody can be the perfect parent. You can only do your best.

How did you find the adoption panel?

Simon: Before our approval panel, I felt a strange mix of nervousness and confidence. Nervous that we couldn't really know how it would go, but confident that we had done all we could, and that we knew that we could make good parents. If anyone had a problem with us, we were prepared to take them on! In a way, the easiest part was when we were in the room being questioned by the panel members. They asked about six questions, like why had we chosen our adoption agency, plus a couple of unexpected ones. It was an agonising wait outside the room while the panel came to their decision. Finally, the panel Chair came and told us that we were approved! At long last we were onto the next stage of our journey, and could talk about "when", not "if", we have children.

10

Karen and Siobhan

Karen and Siobhan have been together for about five years. Karen works with adults with learning disabilities and Siobhan works as a police officer. They have adopted two boys aged two and five with dual heritage. Siobhan tells their story.

Why did you decide to adopt?

My partner cannot have children due to a hysterectomy several years ago. I, on the other hand (as far as I know), *can* have children but was concerned about my age and the higher risk of my birth child having a significant disability. We talked in depth about all the options and felt that this was the best way forward for us as a couple.

What experience did you have of children beforehand?

Karen has eight nieces and nephews with numerous friends whom we regularly look after. I have one niece and one nephew and also have friends who have children we regularly looked after.

How did you decide on the adoption agency you chose?

We researched the options and contacted all of the relevant agencies. We felt that we received a greater deal of support and understanding from our local authority (hence our choice to progress with them).

What was the initial reaction of the adoption agency/ies?

Fantastic! Really surprised how supportive they were, especially since we were the first same-sex couple in our area to make an enquiry.

What was your experience of the preparation course?

Very positive and we have kept in touch with several of the couples/singles that were at the course.

How did you decide on your preference, for example, adopting siblings, and the ages and sex of children?

We both wanted a boy, but during the home study our social worker intimated that she felt we were suitable for siblings. We thought about it and felt that this was a good option. We wanted a young child/children in order that we could spend some time with him/them getting used to having two mummies prior to attending school.

What was your experience of the home study?

Very positive, we were very fortunate in the choice of social worker allocated to us, we all hit it off immediately and she totally gets us.

What was your experience of the adoption panel?

Very helpful and friendly.

What advice would you give to anyone going through these stages?

Try and take each day as it comes, try to be patient, be honest about everything (especially to your partner), and be yourself.

What was your experience of finding a match?

Our match happened within a week of approval; very obviously we had been considered prior to that date. The match was perfect. The boys are everything we could have dreamed of and more. They are brothers aged two and five, with dual heritage and no disabilities.

What was your experience of meeting the children?

Very emotional and extremely nerve-racking. The foster carers and social workers were looking at us playing with the children, which was such an alien feeling. We had three long weeks of introductions, which we felt was too long and involved loads of travelling.

What was it like in the first stages of settling in as a family?

It was very tiring but rewarding. The foster carer did an excellent job with night-time routines/meal times and lots of last minute shopping.

What emotional and behavioural issues have you had to deal with?

The two-year-old has been a bit grumpy, which wasn't helped by him banging heads with another child at a soft play area recently. The five-year-old has been good, a bit hyper and does need a certain amount of reassurance.

Have you had any contact with birth parents and family?

No.

What has been your experience of dealing with the following?

School

Excellent – they have bent over backwards for us. Our choice of school is not in our catchment area. My advice would be to contact the school and meet with the head teacher to get a tour, check the facilities and support available, if required, and ask to meet your child's teacher. Get involved with the community – Karen is now a member of the PTA. This affords the opportunity to meet the parents and get involved in your child's education.

Friends and family

They are very supportive. Our family are very for us anyway and the gay aspect was never an issue. To be honest, most of them anticipated that we would (at some stage) start a family. We talked through all the stages with them and involved them all in certain aspects. For example, my mother (who is an artist) designed and made the family book.

Discussing your sexuality with the children

We have mentioned a few things to our oldest, bringing more things into the conversation on a gradual basis. We also show affection in front of the children. We read a great deal of books about other same-sex couples' experiences and also the experiences of children of same-sex couples. The internet is also an invaluable tool.

Ethnicity

One of our friends has a mixed-race boy of the same age as our oldest and we have discussed this with him. We found that it came up anyway when we discussed different family dynamics.

The foster family

We plan to keep in contact with the foster carers and regularly send texts. This is a difficult one to give advice on as you either bond with them or not. I wasn't too keen on the male foster carer but I think you have to be aware of the bigger picture and bite your tongue at times. The female carer was wonderful and all credit to her.

Making a photo album/video to introduce yourselves to the child/ren

We really enjoyed making the "forever family book" and commissioned my mother, who is an artist, which involved her in the process.

Playing one parent off against another

We discuss this regularly with the oldest and each other. Children can be quite crafty and, if in doubt, check with your partner to check that you are not being played.

Setting boundaries

It has been very important for the oldest and we have set clear boundaries from the start. We do, however, have to regularly mention things to the oldest as he does test the boundaries on occasion.

Dealing with children's homophobia

The oldest was apparently very surprised about getting two mummies. We have been discussing our sexuality regularly with him and there have been no issues at the moment.

Leave from work, employers' and colleagues' attitudes

My work was great – I got four-and-a-half week's "paternity" leave. Karen's work didn't have an adoption policy in place. However, when challenged, they got their act together. The excuse was 'We haven't had anyone apply for adoption leave in 30 years!'

Attachment disorder

Not a problem as our two attached very quickly. It has to be at their pace and this can be frustrating at times but the trick is patience. It is all worth it in the end. Our boys are so affectionate.

Effect on your own relationship and sex life

Sex? What's that? I jest, everything is great, we talk a lot and still wander about naked.

Post-adoption support

I have our social worker's mobile, house phone and e-mail address but haven't needed it yet. The kids' key worker visits regularly too.

Training provided

The preparation group was really invaluable, apart from that, we apparently didn't need any other training.

11

Max and Craig

Max and Craig, who are white, adopted two white boys, aged five and six, in 2004. This was before the law changed allowing couples to adopt, so Max was the "legal" adopter, although they have brought them up as a couple from day one. They are both teachers and live in London. Max tells their story.

Why did you decide to adopt?

I'm a primary school teacher and have taught a few children who have had horrendous home experiences and some who have been in care and always thought it would be nice to have children and give them a good home.

Our borough council placed advertisements on bus stops saying they were looking for gay and lesbian adoptive parents. They were obviously quite keen to attract gay couples and had children who needed parents.

It took about three years in total with an 18-month gap between approval and the children being placed. We had a really decent social worker. Although the process was slow, she stayed with our case the whole way through. Often they change jobs or move away, so it can be difficult.

What was your experience of the home study?

We had some very probing and testing questions in the home study about our relationship, sex life and previous partners. They also asked how much we drink. Sometimes, it was more like a therapy session.

I would say before you even start the process, get some experience of looking after children. We are teachers, so we had a lot but teaching is still different from parenting. We did a lot of babysitting for our friends to get some more experience. It can be difficult to have this access if not many of your friends have children.

You need to talk about issues as a couple beforehand and decide how you are going to handle the process. We had a mutual opt-out clause, so if one of us wasn't happy at any stage, we could talk about it and pull out if necessary.

It's also sensible to have been together for a while, as it does change your relationship. It can test you to the limit. You have to know each other well and be heading in the same direction.

Once you start the process, you are very much in the hands of the social workers – the ones who represent you and those representing the children. They are very powerful and may also have prejudices or preconceptions. One told us that children "need a mother", two others had a very superficial understanding of gay relationships. It's not necessarily homophobia, just ignorance.

Early on you have to choose two referees. I would choose a referee who has children of their own so they know how you are with their children. I think it's fine to choose straight or gay friends but be aware that some of your gay friends may not welcome the idea of gay adoption. We had a number of friends who thought it was a bad idea but I think it reflects their own feelings about sexuality.

On this note, if you can't be open about your sexuality in all areas, you shouldn't be thinking about adoption. Your children will have to get through school with kids saying stuff and they need to have a clear message from home that we are OK. You shouldn't ever expect the children to hide your sexuality or keep secrets. It is also important that you are out at work as there will be times when you have to leave work if the children are ill. You will also then get your entitlement to adoption leave.

What was your experience of finding a match?

Once we were approved, we had to go through magazines like *Be My Parent* and ring up if there were children we wanted to adopt. We were looking for two boys between four and nine.

The boys we eventually adopted were living in the north of England so our introductions were concentrated into a two-week period, with us staying in a hotel. Before meeting the children, we were shown photographs of the children and the forms detailing their life story. We also met their social worker and foster parents. If you just read the form, you could be put off as they had already been in two adoptive families but it was because the placements weren't appropriate rather than anything to do with the children.

The foster parents weren't too sure about us adopting the children to start with, but they were fine once they met us and we explained how we would look after the children. We then met the children and it was a weird experience, walking in and thinking these could be your future children. It was very artificial. The children came to visit us before they moved in.

What was it like in the first stages of settling in as a family?

You don't always know how much the children have been told. We don't think ours had been properly prepared. Shortly after they moved in, they asked if we were brothers. The social worker said she had explained but maybe they hadn't taken it on board or didn't really understand.

We have tried to be involved in any groups of adoptive gay families, so they don't feel too isolated.

I had six months off and then worked part-time when the children first arrived. You have to be prepared that work comes second and you have to make sacrifices. Even if they are at school age, you have to be there for them. Your career is going to be affected.

We did get a lump sum from the council to help the children settle in, buying beds, etc, and also a weekly payment for six months, which was supposed to replace lost income.

It's important for the children to have a line to tell other children in the playground. One of our children used to tell anyone everything. You don't want them to lie but you have to teach them to use common sense about how much you disclose to people.

To begin with, a lot of people seeing us at the school gates assumed we were two straight dads picking up our sons. It does intrigue kids and some of their friends have asked questions, which we answer honestly. I think the main tension any children experience is the difference between home culture and school culture. At home, being gay is fine and we talk about it quite openly, but at school, gay is used as a term of abuse.

I feared our children might reject us but they've never said anything negative to our faces and seem to have embraced being part of a gay family. I think they will grow up differently not having a female influence in the home but then lots of kids grow up without a male influence. Studies have shown that there isn't any detrimental effect on children growing up in a gay family. I don't think there is any more likelihood of them being gay or straight.

I think some adopted children can be attention seeking, quite bold and brassy with a kind of brittle toughness and a soft underneath. If you are a birth child, you know where you come from and you never question it – things are more certain. But with adoptive children, they know from a very young age that adults can be unreliable. It can take time for them to build up trust.

When they first moved in, my partner and I had a de-briefing every night about what the children were doing, how we were reacting, did we do it right. We went into a lot of detail but it seemed necessary. It is a big learning experience and you will get things wrong, you just have to go on your instincts.

I used to think the world was divided between gay and straight and now I think it's divided between those with kids and those without. I've realised how hard it is to be a parent.

What has been your experience of dealing with various issues?

Your relationship

Having children puts a lot of pressure on your relationship and you have to face things you haven't ever encountered before. It changes your relationship, particularly the amount of time you have for each other. There was one time when I felt like walking away but I realised that all the issues they were bringing up were to do with me, they were provoking me but they were my issues.

Playing one parent off against the other

The children tried to polarise us into good daddy, bad daddy. Good daddy who buys things, bad daddy who makes us tidy up. They tried to provoke responses they have had before, for example, they had been smacked by previous carers, so behaved badly to try to provoke us into doing the same. Previous carers had also shown favouritism between them, so we had to be religiously fair when buying anything for them or handing out praise to undo that pattern.

Beliefs and feelings

They also projected on to us their feelings. You have to sit back and think, am I feeling angry or am I picking up their anger?

It also makes you think quite hard about what you really believe in because you have to tell them what you think about things, for example, whether God made the world.

Friends and family

Having children transforms your relationship with your own parents. It makes you realise that you are either copying what they did or rejecting their methods. I think you should think about your own childhood quite a bit in the preparation because when you have children of your own you are sucked back into a hideous time warp of your own childhood.

For example, my older brother dominated me and I can't bear it if I see our older child being rough with his brother. I also desperately wanted piano lessons when I was a child. We organised lessons for our children and they weren't interested. You have to realise that is to do with you and not them. It is quite therapeutic, revisiting your own childhood. Sometimes it is lovely and nostalgic but sometimes it is quite scary. It is extremely powerful, seeing yourself in the parent role and remembering being a child hearing your parents saying the same thing to you.

By adopting older children, they arrive with full-blown personalities from day one. With a birth child, you have nine months preparation and then see them grow up from babies.

Our parents have accepted them as grandchildren but I think the birth grandchildren in the family are treated more favourably. I think this is to do with my mother not really coming to terms with me being gay. If there is any hostility in the family, the children have to come first. We made the decision that if anyone had negative attitudes, we just wouldn't go round to their house with the children. We have also had to take that decision with their friends' parents. If anyone is going to say anything hostile, they aren't allowed to go back to that friend's house.

I think we were a slight novelty when the children started school because the other parents tended to know each other from Natural Childbirth Trust classes all the way through nursery and primary school. We haven't encountered any hostility. There is a much bigger commonality of being parents. It is strange suddenly being propelled into the predominantly straight world of playgrounds, etc. Generally speaking, it is an enriching experience. It can actually seem quite alien when you go back into the gay world, which can seem quite shallow. That sounds judgemental but it is probably because people in gay bars will tend to be younger and not have children. The gay world isn't very child-friendly, it is too expensive and people don't expect you to turn up to a gay restaurant with children.

One of the things that struck me when we first had the children was how much time parents sacrifice for their children, standing around pushing a swing or waiting while they play in the park.

Our children say they want to get married and have children, even as young as 18, maybe because they didn't have a very good early start. It is quite common for adopted children to want to heal their own wounds by recreating a family. So we'll probably be there with the contraceptives, saying, wait a while before you do!

Other advice

Ask your social worker to arrange a meeting with any other gay couples in your area who have adopted.

Get out early if it's really difficult. Be realistic about what you can manage.

Some things are easier with adoption; people who might have an issue with gay people having birth children can see it as a social good.

Often people see adoption as a last resort after trying to have children naturally. I don't think adoption is second best.

We would definitely recommend it. Despite all the challenges, it is worth it.

12

Lucia and Abigail

Lucia and Abigail adopted two girls, one from South America and one from the UK. Lucia is a psychologist and Abigail is a teacher. They have been together for 14 years and had a civil partnership in 2007. Lucia tells their story.

Why did you decide to adopt?

I always thought I would adopt a child, even before I knew I was gay. In terms of my extended family accepting us as a lesbian couple having children, adoption was easier than artificial insemination. They see adoption as a "good deed", while artificial insemination is seen as bringing children into a less than perfect family.

As Abigail is a teacher, she thought she didn't need her own children, but then she taught several children in care and some who had been adopted and became very involved with their experiences.

We seriously considered fostering to begin with, beginning an assessment for that and briefly working together in a children's home. We soon decided that this was not for us as social services' involvement was too great and we couldn't be the parents we wanted to be.

What experience did you have of children beforehand?

I grew up in a large extended family with three younger siblings and many younger cousins. I had worked in the family assessment/child protection field for quite a few years before our first adoption.

Abigail had always enjoyed working with children, became a primary school teacher and had been doing that for six years before our first adoption.

How did you decide on the adoption agency you chose?

Our first adoption was in Brazil as I'm Brazilian. At the time (1998) we believed that in the UK a lesbian couple would only be considered for very "hard to adopt" children. We had good contacts in Brazil and that seemed like an easy solution. It wouldn't be for a UK couple as they would have to go through international adoption procedures, but I could adopt under Brazilian national law. This involved us moving there and being resident for a year.

Our second adoption was in Brighton and Hove. It took three years in total. We moved to Brighton because it is such a gay-friendly city, and became aware that same-sex couples were much more favourably viewed here than we had thought.

What was the initial reaction of the adoption agencies?

In Brazil, we were not "out" at all! I adopted as a single parent.

In Brighton and Hove, the local authority was very positive. We had the sense that they felt it was an asset to have lesbian and gay adopters and wanted to promote this.

What was your experience of the preparation course?

We felt they over-simplified some difficulties, for example, saying, 'Be prepared that your children may never be able to love you', rather than 'It might take lots of thought and work to help your children to love you but it is possible'.

How did you decide on your preference, for example, the age and sex of children?

First adoption: We were not very clear about age or gender preference. At one point we thought we would bring two children back – a young child and a baby. We were sent pictures of some children from a children's home and fell in love with our elder daughter through those pictures. She was three-and-a-half by the time she was placed with us.

Second adoption: We began the second process two years after our first daughter was placed. By now this was going quite well, and we felt comfortable with adopting another toddler – up to around three years. We had concerns about adopting a baby as these are much more of a mystery – you know so much less about how they are actually developing and what problems may be hidden. However, we did not want an older child who was already at school and who would not have enough time with us at home. Gender did not matter but we ended up being matched with another girl.

What was your experience of the home study?

In our experience, the aim of the home study was for social services to "vet" us as parents, rather than to help us genuinely reflect on and learn about parenting/adoption issues. We didn't find it useful and we didn't think it was a very good vetting tool, as it quickly became apparent that you needed to say the right things and tick the right boxes rather than express genuine questions, doubts or challenge the social worker. If we did so, the process quickly ground to a halt until we toed the line!

It could be useful for social services to separate the process – having one social worker do the vetting, while another provides a safe space to really explore difficult and challenging issues without being afraid that it's all going to be called off. It is almost impossible to really trust or be open with the assessing social worker, who has the power to make or break the placement. This leads to less openness and a situation of increased risk for all.

This was our experience despite having a lesbian social worker who was extremely positive about us – these concerns must be much greater for those who suspect or experience homophobic social workers.

It would also be useful to separate the process in post-adoption support – you need a source of support who is not also someone who might take the child away. Currently the assessing social worker tends to then become the family social worker after placement, when there is already a huge power dynamic in place.

What was your experience of the adoption panel?

In terms of working with a lesbian couple the panel was fine – in fact, in keeping with the general Brighton and Hove approach, they seemed particularly positive and supportive of us as lesbian adopters.

What advice would you give to anyone going through these stages?

Be prepared for a rollercoaster, and to surrender control to people you might not respect. Grit your teeth and get through it! At the same time, make sure you do have some safe space to genuinely reflect on things that come up. You want to become aware of what you really feel, want and what you are getting into when adopting a child. Fears, expectations – you need to be pretty realistic about all that – but explore it safely first and then tell your social worker!

What was your experience of finding a match?

It took a long time, and then the reasons we were matched were laughable – our second daughter is mixed-race – one-eighth from a country in the same continent as Brazil! This was enough of a link to count. We didn't argue…

Please describe the children you have adopted.

Both girls, both three at the time of placement (though five years apart). One Brazilian, of mixed heritage. The second is British, also of mixed heritage. Neither have disabilities.

What was your experience of meeting the children?

In Brazil it felt a little more comfortable as we felt less closely scrutinised by the staff at the children's home – we were left to get on with it and were more relaxed and more aware of what we were feeling. In Brighton, we felt under observation and self-conscious. These first few encounters are so loaded and take on a disproportionate importance, a bit like a driving test: you really learn to drive once you have passed and are doing it yourself. You really get going with the child once they are in your home and you are being their parent.

What was it like in the first stages of settling in as a family?

It's a blur, probably a bit like giving birth! Some bits are a nightmare, others are wonderful but you are just so caught up in getting through it that it's hard to take stock of what is happening. The emotions of all parties are so powerful and complex, yet at the same time we were trying to control them, so you can have surreal "normal" moments, interspersed with completely mad ones. The mad ones feel more real at the time.

There is also a fear of being exposed to the outside world in this state – and trying to put up a façade of things working. This is more so in the UK with social services visits, and the fear that they might even interrupt the placement if you share too many problems.

What are some things that helped or worked for you?

Taking time off to spend time with the child without work pressure. For both adoptions, we worked less than one full-time job between the two of us for the first six months to a year. I would really want to stress to prospective adopters that they plan to take as much or more time off as they would if they had a biological baby – or twins! Don't imagine that just because a child is of nursery or school age, you can go back to work sooner…you need time and energy to bond! The transition of adoption is huge and traumatic for children and it is important to acknowledge and support a child through this, reading the signs as and when they are ready, rather than try to lull a child into a false sense of everything should be normal, leading to suppression of the feelings of grief.

A child is not settling in well just because they get through the daily routines well. They are settling in when they are able to begin to express and process all the difficult feelings – this will take years, and is a wonderful and rewarding process.

Looking out for, being prepared for and even encouraging the expression of difficult "real" emotions such as fear, confusion, rejection, sadness, anger, etc, rather than trying to foster the false "happy family" image.

Working hard on creating/fostering attachment and appropriate dependence. Even what seems like age-appropriate independence in a toddler or older child is not appropriate if trying to create an attachment, so we encouraged co-sleeping with a mattress on the floor of our bedroom, and did not use babysitters for a year. With our second daughter we did a very gradual introduction to nursery – less than she had been used to. With our first daughter we regretted sending her to nursery for the kinds of hours she had been used to. We wished we had kept her more at home.

Have you had any contact with birth parents and family – what was that like?

With our first daughter, we maintain yearly contact with her birth family in Brazil. This has been a complex process, full of ups and downs, but definitely invaluable for her. She (now 12) is aware of her own confusing and ambivalent emotions, but these are crucial to her identity as an adopted child. Although contact trips are very draining for all of us, they are also incredibly strengthening of our bond with her as well as of her bond with her birth family.

Our second daughter comes from a local family, and although her biological mother is dead, contact with her biological grandmother is so much easier than going to Brazil! We have now established a relaxed and relatively frequent contact – regular special events such as school assemblies, birthday, Christmas, etc. After three years, they have also begun to take her out by herself – this is because she now feels ready for this.

Contact with both girls' fathers has been more complicated. Neither girl ever lived with their father. Our younger daughter has letterbox contact. Both girls are very aware of this missing part of their lives. They may go for months without mentioning it but we sense it is always there.

13

Liam and Chris

Liam and Chris, a white couple, have been matched with a boy aged two, who is also white. Chris is from North America and is a teacher. Liam is English and works in the media. They are both in their thirties and have been married for three years. Liam tells their story.

Why did you decide to adopt?

Chris and I had talked about parenting for a long time and had explored the different options available to us. It took us a while to come to adoption, because we weren't sure whether we were ready to take on the responsibility of full-time parenting. We were also uncertain about the kind of child we would have to parent. We didn't know anyone else in our position who was doing the same thing. And we weren't sure we were ready to have our lives picked over by social services.

But once we realised we did want to be full-time parents, adoption made a lot of sense. A major catalyst was meeting up with an old friend who was planning to adopt with his partner. They had put calls in to a few councils and talking to them made a scary concept seem possible. And they also led us to a gay adopters' social group, New Family Social, where we met other gay mums and dads who had adopted, along with others in the same boat as us, who wanted to.

It was a revelation to see children playing happily, who had been placed with a same-sex couple, and who seemed entirely at ease with the idea of having two dads or mums.

What experience did you have of children beforehand?

Apart from being an instructor at summer camp in America when I was 19, I had very little experience with children in my adult life. My partner Chris, who's a teacher, obviously has a great deal. But when we approached our London borough as prospective adopters, they insisted that I get extra experience before they would take us on. So it was a question of working out what I could do to gain that experience.

Fortunately, Chris's job meant we had contacts in the world of education. He used to teach at a local primary school and so we asked the head teacher if I could help out one morning a week in the nursery class. I am very lucky as I don't have a traditional nine to five job. I asked if I could be rostered to have Wednesday mornings off for almost the entire academic year, and despite being petrified on my first day at the nursery, I really enjoyed building up a relationship with the three- and four-year-olds.

I also found it immensely useful, as I was paired with the head of the Early Years Unit, who had been in the line of work for 25 years. By observing how she dealt with discipline issues, I learnt a lot about how to deal with difficult behaviour and this served me well when we went back to our borough and talked about the experience I had gained.

Apart from that, we borrowed the children of any friends who were willing to lend them to us. It was quite an interesting process, considering which friends had children in the right age range, and whether they would let us look after their beloved offspring.

Luckily enough, we had very positive responses. We looked after one couple's four-year-old son, spending weekends with them, where they would go out and we would feed and bathe him and put him to bed. In the morning we would look after him while his parents had a well-deserved lie-in. We would take him out too, not just to fun places like adventure playgrounds, but the supermarket.

Another friend had just given birth to a daughter, who was six weeks old when I first met her. I didn't think it was likely we would be matched with a child that young but I thought that the experience would serve me well as I felt it would be useful to know what life was like for a child in the very early days. It involved a lot of carrying and soothing when she was unhappy, nappy changing of course, and more and more play as the months went on.

How did you decide on the adoption agency you chose?

Our East London borough was recommended to us as gay-friendly, so we thought we'd give them a try, even though they're our own local authority. Many people prefer to go with a different local authority so there's no chance of bumping into the birth parents on the high street. But ultimately you don't have to take a child from the authority that approves you, and even if we were to do this, we live right on the edge of the borough, so encountering our child's birth parents would be unlikely. We did approach a few other councils in London, where we live. Picking up the phone the first time to admit to someone in authority that we wanted to adopt was surprisingly hard. I felt nervous – it was like nothing else I'd ever done before.

One local authority told me they were closed to white parents; others were a little more positive, saying we could come along to an adopters' evening. But our borough somehow sounded the most encouraging so we went with them. And we weren't disappointed. At our first meeting, they were at pains to make clear they regard same-sex couples as the same as straight couples. They explained that the belief that gay adopters would only get matched with "difficult" children was outdated. And we even found articles on the internet written by the first social worker we met talking about the acceptance of gay adopters in the borough.

What was your experience of the preparation course?

The preparation course took place on three consecutive Tuesdays and one Saturday and was interesting and even fun at times. It seemed ours was a breeze compared to the experiences of friends. It's important to remember that the people running the course are assessing you throughout, so you have to participate eagerly and show knowledge and insight about the issues being discussed. But we didn't have people sitting in the background constantly taking notes, as friends of ours did.

We were the only gay couple in a group of five couples. Two of the other couples were a little older than us, and were foster carers looking to adopt children that they were already looking after.

One of the couples were Jehovah's Witnesses and the other were salt of the earth East End types, so we weren't sure how they would react to us as a gay couple, but they were more than friendly. Everyone got along very well, although one of the things you are supposed to demonstrate on the course is tolerance of others, so we all knew we had to be on our best behaviour!

What was your experience of the home study?

The home study period was intense and happened over a period of five months – well within the government's stipulation of eight months. We were very happy with the way our social worker kept on making appointments and addressed all the questions that the Form F asks.

Each visit probably lasted an average of three hours and at first it was a bit like free therapy, getting to talk about yourself, your childhood and so on. Our social worker wanted to go into quite a bit of detail at times, which sometimes got a bit boring! We developed an understanding of each other's personalities and got along quite well.

How did you decide on your preference, for example, adopting siblings, or the ages and sex of children?

We ended up going to panel asking to be approved for a boy under four years. We came to that specification after talking to our social worker. We wanted a young child, and she suggested that age range would be realistic for us. Originally we had said 0 to 5 years, but she encouraged us to revise the upper limit downwards after getting the impression from us that we wouldn't be that willing to adopt a child older than five.

Chris and I settled on asking for a boy for a number of reasons. We both had brothers growing up and I felt more comfortable understanding what it's like for a boy to grow up than a girl. We felt we would probably have more to offer a boy than a girl, although it's only a slight preference, and we wouldn't have any problem with raising a girl. We're also aware from talking to friends that whom you're approved for at panel often has no resemblance to the child that ultimately is placed with you!

What was your experience of adoption panel?

We had been told that the panel was a formality and that we would have never got this far if we didn't think we were going to get through. But it turned out to be the most fraught part of the process. When the date of the panel came, we turned up to the town hall and waited for what seemed like ages while the panel discussed our case next door. Eventually the panel head came out and talked to us reassuringly. Our social worker went in first. We were expecting to follow her but when she came out the panel head said, 'I'm afraid there's been a problem...' In that instant, my heart was in my throat. This had departed from the script. Was the year of effort that we had put into getting here about to be wasted?

It turned out there had been a discrepancy in our Form F. We guessed something one of our referees had said contradicted our narrative. But because the referees' words are confidential, they couldn't tell us exactly what the problem was. It was extremely frustrating, even though we were reassured that they should be able to sort out the problem, and that we would be invited back when the panel next met in two weeks' time.

It was a long time to wait, but the problem was sorted out, and two weeks later we were brought in front of the panel. They seemed nice and asked us a few questions, including why we wanted a boy, whether we had people nearby we could call on in an emergency, and if we knew other gay parents. It didn't last very long and almost as soon as we left the room, the head of the panel followed us out to tell us we'd been approved. It was a life-changing moment and Chris, our social worker and I hugged each other.

What was your experience of finding a match?

We were approved for a child under four, and the experience of going through publications like *Children Who Wait* and *Be My*

Parent helped us narrow down what we were looking for even more. As we considered each case, we felt more inclined to look for a child aged two or three. We had always been open to accepting a baby, but we didn't feel the need to parent a child from as near birth as possible, as I believe some straight adopters, who have wrestled with issues of infertility, may feel. I think many gay adopters feel the same way, and are therefore an asset to social services in accepting older children who are traditionally harder to place.

It's harrowing to read the Child's Permanence Reports (CPRs) and find out about their troubled backgrounds. We were told by friends to be proactive, approach children's social workers ourselves, and be prepared for a few "no"s. As it happened, we were surprised how quickly our match came. About two months after getting approved, we were matched with a two-and-a half-year-old boy and the matching panel and introductions were scheduled for about two or three months after that.

14

Suzie and Jane

Suzie and Jane, who are both white, adopted a 13-month-old baby girl, who is also white. Their child is now four. She has Foetal Alcohol Syndrome. Suzie is 36 and Jane is 39. Suzie used to work with adults with complex needs, until she gave up her job to look after their daughter. Jane is a housing support manager. They have been together for nearly 15 years and had a civil partnership three years ago. Suzie tells their story.

Why did you decide to adopt?

We wanted to start a family and looked briefly into sperm donation but decided the success rate was too low to risk. So we started to look into adoption.

What experience did you have of children beforehand?

Jane, my other half, has two nephews and a niece. I had little experience but I had done a little work within a special needs school, which I loved.

How did you decide on the adoption agency you chose?

We approached three local authorities. We were accepted by two of these and we choose the one with the most relaxed social workers.

What was the initial reaction of the adoption agency/ies?

The first local authority used every excuse, except the fact that we were gay. They said there was no way we would ever get a child as our bathroom was downstairs! The next two local authorities who visited us thought this was hilarious and of course said it was no problem. The local authority we chose, which is in the north of England, was fabulous. The only negative thing they said was that, as a lesbian couple, we would never get a baby.

What was your experience of the preparation course?

We really enjoyed it. It was fun and informative and the social workers were great. There was loads of role-play and interaction. They had a fabulous birth mother come in and tell us her story, which was amazing. Also loads of adoptive parents and foster carers.

How did you decide on your preference, for example, adopting siblings, or the ages and sex of children?

We always knew our preference was for a girl, but we did decide as the home study went on that we would accept up to two girls. Jane always wanted a child as young as possible but I would have gone up to 15, so we met in the middle somewhere and were approved for one to two girls up to the age of six or a boy with Down's Syndrome.

What was your experience of the home study?

Again, we both enjoyed it. We had a fabulous social worker. She was more like a friend. She was really open and honest so when we were discussing our personal life stories she also told us loads about herself so it never felt one-way. For us it never felt all that intrusive but I can imagine with a more closed social worker it must feel like it is.

What was your experience of the adoption panel?

Bloody scary – we arrived at the Civic Centre, a big cold place, and sat in the corridor for what felt like an eternity. We then went into a room to be faced by ten people, they went through our form and then asked us to leave the room. They then asked us back in and posed a couple of questions (the inevitable male role model question) and asked us to leave again. They called us back in and said it was a unanimous yes...I then burst into tears!

What advice would you give to anyone going through these stages?

Where possible, relax – the social workers, panel and everyone else concerned are on your side. They are there to get the right families the right children, so be honest, and don't expect anything to happen too quickly.

What was your experience of finding a match?

We were approved on 14 August and got a phone call five weeks later to tell us they had a little girl for us. The introductions started on 4 November so we had a really quick match, everything went very quickly and smoothly.

Please describe the child you have adopted

We adopted a beautiful baby of 13 months, who is now four. When I set out to adopt I only wanted to be considered for a child with a learning disability, so we got the Form E for a little girl who has Foetal Alcohol Syndrome (FAS). She has developmental delay, epilepsy, poor balance and no sense of danger. She is the most perfect kid in the world.

What was your experience of meeting her?

Strange, to say the least, to walk into someone else's house to meet the love of your life! The foster carer was told by a rubbish social worker that our little one would never find a family due to her needs so she thought she would keep her in long-term foster care, so she was very cold towards us. We walked into her house and saw this beautiful little baby asleep on the floor in a horrible brown dress with snot running down her face and we knew that she was the best thing we would ever do.

What was it like in the first stages of settling in as a family?

Easy really, it all sort of fell into place. We had seven days of introductions and then she moved in and it all sort of seemed normal.

What emotional and behavioural issues have you dealt with?

Because she has FAS, her level of understanding is delayed so she can get quite frustrated when she does not understand, so her mood swings can be quite extreme, biting, nipping and hitting. But on the whole she is quite calm.

Have you had any contact with birth parents and family – what was that like?

We have had annual letterbox contact but until last week we hadn't heard anything back. It was great to receive our first letter and to know the birth mother is thinking about our little one. She asked to see a photo and we felt a bit put on the spot. We had said from the beginning no photos and as she is also a lesbian we were worried she might be able to trace us as the lesbian community is quite small.

We were glad to know she is OK, although obviously she has a drink problem. We met her during introductions. She wasn't what we expected – she was little and sad and ordinary.

What has been your experience of dealing with the following?

School

Fab – she is only at nursery at the moment and has the most brilliant (lesbian) head teacher. She would jump through burning hoops for any of her kids and is fighting like hell to get a statement in place before our little one starts school.

Friends and family

My family have been behind us right from the start. They have never had any issues with my sexuality. They adore the little one and see her every day. Jane's parents were a little slower and were against it at first. They also have issues with her sexuality. They are coming to terms with it now and do accept her as a grandchild, but as they live over 300 miles away they don't see her too often. My advice to anyone would be to do it for yourself, not your family. In time, most people will soften.

Discussing your sexuality with the children

As she is only four this has not come up yet, although hopefully as she has been with us since a baby it will just be the norm for her. Friends who have adopted older children have had no problems with their little one and it is all out in the open.

The foster family

We got off to a pretty bad start with the foster carer but we are now very close. We take the little one to see her every couple of months.

Setting boundaries

Ha ha...I confess I don't very much. I am a soft touch. Jane is slightly stricter. I try to parent in the same way I was parented, so where possible allow the little one to make her own decisions, within reason, of course.

Leave from work, employers' and colleagues' attitudes

We both worked for local authorities so got all our entitlement. I took adoption leave and Jane "paternity", which was a rubbish two weeks. So she had to take a month unpaid, which we had saved for.

Effect on your own relationship

Our relationship has not changed too much, although we probably don't have sex as often as we did – far too tired.

How have you found the post-adoption support on offer?

We are still heavily involved with the local authority we adopted through. They have been fantastic; however, we have not needed them for anything. I do feel confident that the support would be there if we did. They run a support group for adopters, which is about every couple of months. We helped them set up a gay and lesbian support group, which is open to any gay adopters or prospective adopters in the North East of England. The local authority is funding us to attend a Foetal Alcohol Syndrome conference at the end of this month.

Overall, I would really recommend it – parenting is great.

15

Richard

Richard is 40 years old and works in a bank. He comes from a large family. He is a keen golfer, runner and swimmer and enjoys participating in these activities with his brothers, sisters, nieces and nephews. Richard has been approved as a single adopter and is looking for a suitable match.

Why did you decide to adopt?

I grew up as part of a large and close-knit family – I was one of a sibling group of six, within a two-parent family. My childhood was a very happy one. There was always so much going on at home. I am the youngest of the six. My brothers and sisters always played with me. I grew up with the full expectation of having a family myself. However, from the first moments of sexual awareness, I realised that I was actually gay. So I quickly realised that I would not be able to father children naturally. This was of course a sad realisation as I approached my late teens and I began to understand what this really meant in terms of my future plans to have a family.

Meanwhile I became an uncle at the age of 14. My eldest niece is now 25. In total, I now have 15 nieces and nephews, including twins. This was an important milestone.

I very quickly became aware of the needs of small children, in terms of not only meeting their physical needs, i.e. the requirement to have food at regular intervals, changing nappies, etc, but also the need to ensure the physical safety of the infant – being aware of the environment that they are in and being pro-active to make sure that they can't harm themselves either during play or when discovering their environment. I was soon babysitting and helping out, so I often had to attend to them when distressed in order to find out what the problem was. I must admit that at the time (I was a teenager) I did this automatically as a chore, but I learned to enjoy it and my siblings trusted me with their children. I was also providing attention and playing with them, in particular helping the twins to learn tricycle/bike riding, and of course I would read bedtime stories regularly. I am still actively involved with all my nieces and nephews.

Two years ago I felt that I had reached a secure and stable position in life – I had paid off the mortgage, finished renovating the house and had some money saved. There was now no reason not to adopt!

What other experience did you have of children and what did you learn from this?

I have been a volunteer worker with children since 1997. One job is for a local transport service, which included taking disabled children on outings and to appointments, and helping their parents to get them out of the house and into the metrocab and supporting them during the duration of the visit, as required.

I have also been a reading partner at a school in East London. The primary purpose of the Reading Partners scheme is to help 9–11-year-olds with their reading. The children are primarily from Bengali and Bangladeshi households, where English is the second language and some parents are not able to read English, so can't help their children practise at home. However, initially most of the time prior to starting the reading is spent talking to the children, and developing a bond with them so that they can relate to us and trust that we are friends. The children tell us what they have been doing since we last saw them. It gives us a chance to get to know them better and, very importantly, to have an adult take an interest in what they have been doing and give them some encouragement and support.

How did you decide on the adoption agency you chose?

I didn't have a lot of information on adoption agencies when I started looking into becoming a substitute parent. I started with my local authority, but they were not taking on any new applicants at the time. So I went to the next authority, the one that was geographically closest. I knew the process involved home visits, so it didn't make sense to apply to authorities that were too far away. I also lived in the borough when I was younger and I just felt comfortable contacting them.

What was the initial reaction of the adoption agency/ies?

The first agency I approached took over one month to get back to me. This was a bit disappointing and turned out to be wasted time, as I didn't proceed with any other enquiries during this time.

My experience was much more positive with the south London borough I approached, who seemed to take a more efficient approach. They were keen to meet me. At first they were reluctant to invite me onto the preparation course, saying that I didn't have enough experience with caring for children. This was down to miscommunication on my part, which was resolved quickly – I had omitted to tell them about my voluntary work with children. I was so keen to ask questions of the social worker who came to see me, I think I forget to sell myself well enough!

What was your experience of the preparation course?

I thoroughly enjoyed the preparation course. It was quite intense and participation in the role-plays, exercises, etc, was compulsory. However, it was my first real taste of high-quality information about what it really means to adopt children and how the process fits together. I was especially interested to learn about the problems that children in care face, including the reasons why they come to the point of being separated from their families in the first place, the challenges they face during the process, and how to help them get over the loss and separation issues they have faced.

I felt very welcome at the group. There was one other single applicant – a woman. The social workers were very accommodating and I never felt excluded as a single participant. If a task involved discussing something with "your partner", the task was modified so that the single applicants could participate.

I particularly enjoyed meeting the other applicants. It was interesting to hear their experiences and views. Some had birth children, one couple had previously adopted. I have stayed in touch with the single woman and I have become good friends with one couple. They have been amazingly supportive to me during the assessment and we plan to do lots together with the children in the future. I rank them amongst the nicest and most intelligent people that I have met. Their ability to love and care is inspirational.

It was interesting to share and hear about other peoples' reasons for being childless. I did notice that for some of them the pain associated with this was still very raw (i.e. recent miscarriages, failed IVF, etc). Whereas I came to terms with childlessness so long ago, it was less of an issue for me and I felt that I was starting the process from a very strong and stable position in that regard.

The month went very quickly and was certainly an eye-opener. There were many considerations that I hadn't even thought about. I felt there was a high degree of honesty about both the good things and the potential pitfalls and problems that can be associated with adopting children in care.

How did you decide on your preference, for example, adopting siblings, or the ages and sex of children?

As a single parent, I am very keen to adopt a sibling group of two, of either sex and between the ages of three and eight. I am particularly keen to take two children, as I think it would be more fun for them. They will also have each other as support and that should help them move on from the problems they have faced in the past. I think this is even more important when you are a single parent. There will inevitably be times when I am busy preparing meals or doing other tasks and can't focus on them, and they will have each other to play with. Being part of a large family, we are well able to accommodate large numbers on family get-togethers, etc, and I have two spare bedrooms. So, from a practical perspective I have the necessary facilities. I feel I have the ability/capacity to cope with two, possibly even able to accommodate a sibling group where one child has mild learning difficulties.

What was your experience of the home study?

When I first saw the Form F, I thought it all looked a bit daunting! Especially since I was facing this as a single applicant. I got on very well with my social worker, which was a real blessing. I was especially grateful to him, for several reasons. Firstly, the home study took longer than usual. My first thought was that as I was the first single male carer that the borough have assessed, they would be doubly careful to make sure that they didn't miss anything and covered all the angles. My social worker has said that the report will be longer and more detailed than normal. However, I don't think that is actually the reason. During the home visits, my social worker spent a lot of time discussing issues surrounding the care of children. I found this very informative and helpful. He is a senior social worker and it was clear that he has a wealth of experience to draw from.

Secondly, my social worker gave me some very useful pointers on how to engage friends and family members as part of my support network. He also suggested that I did a stint in a nursery to get some more experience with younger children, as my youngest niece is now 10 years old.

The stint at nursery in itself opened other doors. I met the parent liaison officer who runs family strengthening courses for parents at the school and organises trips and visits as part of the work. She is herself an adoptive parent of four children, has sat on adoption panels and is now on the adoption independent review panel. She has given me so much advice and support and got me involved in a special needs swimming group, where I have met several children in care, who are waiting to be adopted. So my social worker's suggestion has proved amazingly fruitful. This will of course all be relevant and helpful at panel for me.

16

Belinda and Fiona

Belinda is 27 years old and Fiona is 29 years old. They are both public sector workers – Belinda is an administrator and Fiona is a project support worker. They have been together for eight years and are in the early stages of the adoption process.

Why did you decide to adopt?

I had read about a Channel 4 documentary called 'Wanted: A new mum and dad', and decided to watch it based on the fact that I love interesting documentaries. The idea of adoption had never really crossed my mind as a possibility or an option for us and we had previously thought we might go down the sperm donor route.

We watched the documentary together and it featured two gay men who had adopted a young boy. It was my first real knowledge of gay adoption in the UK (though I had read a little bit about it in the book, *A Family Affair*, which I had bought as we were thinking about donor insemination). The laws hadn't changed at this point but were just about to, and I think I hadn't realised that it would soon be possible for gay couples to adopt jointly.

Well, this programme really got us thinking, and we talked about it a lot. It just seemed to make sense and we wondered why we hadn't considered it before. Within a week or two, I had made an initial enquiry via our local authority's adoption website, and received a positive reply, though it wasn't until two years later that we actually decided to set the ball in motion.

What experience did you have of children beforehand?

I have always known that I wanted to be a parent one day. I love children and had done some voluntary work with them in the past, with the ambition of becoming a primary school teacher, though decided not to follow that career path in the end. My experience was limited (and still is, somewhat) and that of my partner was even more limited, although she had worked with older children for a while.

How did you decide on the adoption agency you chose?

We just had a gut feeling about it, really. We had received such a warm welcome in the emails, phone calls and at the information session they invited us to. They were a very friendly and positive team – but there was a catch. There would be a long waiting list to start the assessment process and this applied to everyone.

We did make enquiries with a neighbouring local authority and a voluntary agency, but in the end decided to stick with our local authority as we had a really good feeling about them. We thought we might as well use the wait to our advantage and take care of some things that needed taking care of, such as securing a permanent job and completing work on our house.

What was the initial reaction of the adoption agency/ies?

When we made our initial enquiry to our local authority's adoption team, the social worker who emailed me responded to my message with a very reassuring tone, assuring me that yes, they would accept an application from a same-sex couple (as that had been my question), and told me that they had made some wonderful placements with same-sex couples over the last few years. This reassured me instantly.

Eight months later, I sent another email to them as I had a query about something, and the same social worker who had emailed me months beforehand phoned me at home for a chat. He was extremely friendly and I found him instantly likeable. He seemed completely unfazed and the focus was on our qualities and our environment, not on our sexual orientation. I got a very good feeling from him.

Over a year later, we were finally ready to kick things into action, and made contact with our local authority for the third time. Again, they were very professional and friendly, and warm and welcoming too.

17

Lorraine

Thirteen years ago, Lorraine adopted an eight-year-old girl. Lorraine is now 60 and semi-retired from a career in local government. She has a history of involvement in feminism and women's liberation. She lives in Yorkshire and still looks after her daughter, who is now a student. She tells her story.

Why did you decide to adopt?

I never wanted to be a biological mother but I wanted the experience of being a mother. I was in my forties when I decided to adopt. That was when I had the space in my life. I had been too busy with other things until then. I felt confident that I could love a child that I hadn't given birth to. My ex-partner, who was still living with me, agreed to stay for at least five years to help me bring up a child. We were consciously creating a family, not just with a child but with close and committed friends too.

What experience did you have of children beforehand?

Not very much. I didn't have nieces or nephews and most of my friends didn't have children.

How did you decide on the adoption agency you chose?

I was working for a council in the north of England at the time and trusted that they would do a good job. I went to see the head of the children's services department and he said I would be assessed in the same way as anyone else.

What was your experience of the preparation course?

I enjoyed the training and preparation period. There was a strong emphasis on the fact that a lot of children in care have been sexually abused. I knew about that already because of my political involvements and my ex-partner's job which was in adoption and fostering. I also knew quite a lot of survivors of sexual abuse. However, I think they were stressing it because a lot of the other people on the course were wanting babies with no history to be available for adoption.

What was your experience of the home study?

I found the home study very helpful. It was really important to work through what I could and couldn't cope with. For example, I felt I could work with children who had been abused but not a child who tortured animals or who had eating disorders. In terms of finding a match, I think it is vital to look at why you are adopting, what your own vulnerabilities are and what you are really wanting from the relationship.

The social worker was very good at helping me to discover some of these things and she made a brilliant match. I knew that I wasn't desperate for a baby and wanted to adopt an older child, both for myself and as I knew they were harder to place. I wanted an older child with whom I could communicate verbally and enter into a process.

What did you state as your preference?

I opted for a girl between the ages of 5 and 11. Some people think that the younger the child, the fewer the difficulties, but that is not necessarily the case.

What was your experience of the adoption panel?

In those days, you didn't attend the panel, you just sent in your papers.

What advice would you give to anyone going through these stages?

The skill of the social worker is very important in the matching process. They are making a very sophisticated set of judgments. But, as there are so many children to place, there can be a tendency to try to make things right or not go into all the difficult details in order to place children.

My biggest piece of advice would be to think through what you can cope with and be honest, admit what you can't do, even if it touches on insecurities or things you don't really want to admit to.

There is no point in a bad match that fails for you and the child, so be prepared to say no as there are a lot of other children in foster care that you might be better suited to look after.

What was your experience of finding a match?

We were sent three or four sets of details but there was one who was an obvious match for us. We never felt pressurised. It is very abstract to be considering a child without meeting them. In fact, my social worker allowed me to cheat slightly by visiting the foster carer when the child came home. I wasn't introduced but I saw her.

The moment I laid eyes on her was very scary, seeing how vulnerable and needy she was. I suddenly realised that I could be responsible for this child's life. She had already had two failed adoptive homes and two foster homes. There was a big history and she was not going to be an easy child.

What was your experience of meeting her?

I went to the foster home and there were lots of other kids running around. We were introduced and then Angie went and played in the garden with the other children. Suddenly and of her own free will, she came back in and sat next to me on the sofa and put her head on my shoulder, not saying anything. That was very moving. She then got up and went outside again. I asked her afterwards why she had put her head on my shoulder and she said she felt we had met before.

We had planned for the introductions to take six weeks but we shortened it as we wanted her to move in and she wanted to move in with us. During this time, we put a book together with photos and stories about our lives. This is something she still has and it was useful for her during that introduction time to look at photos of us and our animals and show her friends.

What was it like in the first stages of settling in as a family?

I took a lot of leave and I would recommend this. It is very time- and energy-consuming getting to know a child. I couldn't be at work and be the primary person in her life. In the early stages, we went out every day in the car on trips. My partner, at the time, was very supportive.

What emotional and behavioural issues have you dealt with?

Angie was very, very angry with a huge temper and real fury. I had to learn how to cope with this in the first two years. She was right to be angry about what had happened to her in the past and I never wanted her to get the message that it was not OK to be angry. We also had to learn about things like blowing into a brown paper bag to stop her hyperventilating.

One day she climbed up to the top room and was about to jump out of the window. I just managed to grab her in time. You have to learn very fast. I got her something she could hit but she hit me with it and nearly knocked me down the stairs. I listened to social workers and friends and worked out strategies. Her self-harm was very distressing. She would crush her fingers and cause bruising on her face. I had to go to the school and make sure they knew why she had bruises. I also told the social workers. It is important not to hide anything like this.

She also showed some sexualised behaviour, seeking attention and sitting on laps. We had to deal with that and be very careful about the places and environments she was in, such as the homes and parents of school friends. I bought a book with a lock on it and she told me everything that had happened to her. I wrote it in the book and we locked it up. She needed to be able to keep the memories somewhere but not be troubled by them every day so that she could settle down and have a childhood. She still has that book. I also took her to art therapy and a bit of talking therapy but I'm not sure they did much good.

There were lots of things I didn't know about and needed advice on. For example, it was difficult to know what was the best response when she wanted to get into bed with me. I wasn't sure what to do. I went to see the chief psychiatrist at the council's mental health service and he said to just be natural, so I did and let her join me in bed if she wanted to and there were never any problems. It was just a natural closeness but I had been worried about what other people might think.

One of my biggest worries for her was that her sexualised behaviour or the effects of abuse would come back as a teenager and make good relationships very difficult for her. But she is very strong in herself and good at relationships; she usually chooses gentle, kind men of a similar age to her.

Angie also needed to regress. It was a bit weird her turning into a baby at times doing things like needing to be wrapped in a sheet and rocked to sleep. She also behaved like a toddler for a while at first, screaming when I was out of sight.

We had a legal battle after two years to adopt her. We ended up having to go to the High Court as she hadn't been freed for adoption, and I don't think it happens that way now. We had even thought of running away to New Zealand with her if we didn't win the court case; we were determined not to let her down and we were totally bonded to each other by then. I think if we hadn't won that it could have been the end for her. It was her last chance of the kind of loving family she needed so badly.

Going through the freeing process was very tricky. I am a very strong person but I was having panic attacks. It was very undermining. The courts said I might abuse the child as I was a lesbian and the tabloids were looking for us. We hadn't realised we would be creating a legal precedent when we embarked on it.

We had always agreed to contact with the birth mother. She loved Angie but was an alcoholic and couldn't look after Angie or protect her from her father. Angie had accepted this and when her mother objected to the adoption, Angie didn't want to see her again for a while. She wanted to be adopted by us.

Soon after the court case, her mother died, which was a terrible time. Luckily, Angie had a wonderful grandmother whom we kept in touch with until she died. Angie has some older siblings who she sees sometimes. After the court case we were able to really settle down.

What has been your experience of dealing with the following?

School

Angie's education was very disrupted. She didn't have learning difficulties in the traditional sense but had missed out on building blocks because she was just trying to survive. I wish now that I had insisted on more specific help from the beginning. She was very miserable at senior school so I sent her to a Montessori school for two years. She then went back to the senior school but a year behind. Social services were helpful when I asked for support and they paid for extra maths lessons and are still supporting her through higher education. She has an HND and is now studying for a degree.

Friends and family

My father said he didn't know what to expect but in fact they both adored each other. Most of my friends are lesbian and I like to think she has chosen a collection of aunties from amongst them. My ex-

partner still lives nearby and Angie regards both of us as her
parents.

Discussing your sexuality with the child

She has always known that we were two women who lived
together. When she first came to see our house, we both had
separate bedrooms and she saw my double bed and asked who
slept in there with me. She was trying to work it out. I think she
was much more focused on having a mummy. She was very nervous
about us chucking her out and used to hide behind doors to listen
to our conversation and accused me of having other children that I
wasn't telling her about. There were so many things she carried
from her bad experiences of other families that had to be
understood.

Mostly she has been up front to friends and very comfortable with
our sexuality, certainly as she got older. It hasn't really been a big
issue.

Self-harm

I used to try to hold her, not in a restraining way, but in a way that
calms her down. We also had a special piece of music that we
played and she had her own homeopathy tablets that she could
choose to take herself. I don't know if they worked but it all
seemed to help her to calm down and to learn to take control
herself. I think children need to feel properly secure and to start
liking themselves before they can stop self-harming.

Drugs

Never been a problem.

Children who have been abused – acting out patterns of abuse

I kept a very close eye on her as I worried that she had been made vulnerable to exploitative men by her experiences. I was really shocked that some men seemed to notice her vulnerability in this area, even strangers in the street sometimes reacted in a way I found odd. My partner's brother-in-law helped as he was kindly and safe to have around but kept a proper distance from her. Her sexualised behaviour stopped after a while.

Dealing with homophobia

We live in an area with lots of lesbian families; however, "gay" is still a real insult in school. I have not had anything directed at me and Angie is straight, so hasn't been bullied for being gay.

The foster family

Initially we had no problems when we were adopting – they were co-operative. But later it turned out that some of the children, including Angie, had been badly treated. It took some time before Angie trusted us enough and could speak about it.

That is one thing I would advise – you need to gently make sure that your child can talk to you about anything and be prepared to ask about their past. You will find things that have a huge impact on their sensibilities later in life. For example, Angie had been sent away from two homes without any explanations and with all her things in black plastic bags. This made her very suspicious of us as she expected us to abandon her in that way too. No wonder she was so angry!

You want a new start when your child moves in with you but you also need to know in detail what has happened to them. There will always be more than the social worker ever tells you because they don't want to put you off and sometimes they don't know either. This could be because the child hasn't told them or because of the high turnover of social workers. There were all sorts of things like medical records that got lost and that we never had access to, and it is useful to have them to make sure they have had all their injections and if there are any illnesses or genetic issues you should know about.

I think there are often too many children in foster homes and the children live like a pack. For us, this meant that Angie wasn't very good at being by herself and still isn't, but neither did she know how to behave co-operatively. She'd learned basic survival skills but not important social skills.

Playing one parent off against another

Angie did this. The important thing is to talk to one another all the time and bounce things off each other. I think you need two adults in the household to adopt. It would be very hard to do it on your own. You need a break and you need help. I wrote a detailed diary for the first two years, which was a way of off-loading. You find you obsess about the child and you can't do this with everyone, it's too much for your friends.

Setting boundaries

It is easy to say that you must set boundaries, but you have to work this out individually and you have to be flexible. It will be different from the ideal you might want to achieve at the beginning. You have to learn to live with the child that you actually have and focus on their needs. In terms of boundaries, it was important to mean what you say, and be consistent, but to break the rules on the odd occasions if that seems for the best. Every now and again, I would keep her off school for a day and we would run away together and just do some fun things together and have an adventure.

You have to remember that your child will have had appalling times and experiences and sometimes can't adhere to boundaries. Being very positive with all the things they do try to achieve is a better focus.

Dealing with allegations of abuse

We never had to deal with this but Angie did have a sense of being able to go outside the family for help and that she could use that. Sometimes, in the middle of a big argument, she would threaten to tell the social workers that we were mistreating her, but she never did.

Child's homophobia

We never had to deal with this. In fact, I think we provided a place of safety for her by being two women. It was men who had mistreated her, so two women were positively beneficial. I think this could be the case for other children in the care system. We didn't say we were both mothers. It was very clear that she had one mother and a co-parent. I think it would have been confusing for her to have two mummies. Her needs were so great that us being two women wasn't very important to her compared with her need for security and love. By the time she really understood what lesbians are, she was half-way grown up and it wasn't an issue.

Leave from work, employers' and colleagues' attitudes

I took the maximum adoption leave and stretched it out by going back part-time. Not long after the court case, I took sick leave because of the stress and then was medically retired. I had a very senior management position, which involved a lot of committees and evening work. It was impossible to do it and be the kind of mother I wanted to be to Angie.

While I was still at work, I felt that some people were resentful that I was no longer at their disposal and had to leave at specific times. People were kind but I think also a bit resentful that I wasn't so available and had other priorities. I found it hard to do both.

Child's anger

This is still an issue and I puzzle about how to help her manage it. She can still have enormous tantrums, although not often, but it could be a real problem for her in future relationships. However, she doesn't want to do anything specific about it, like talking to a counsellor. It does get better, however, just with her growing into an adult.

Attachment disorder

This wasn't a problem. She was able to attach to us.

Class

My daughter is resolutely working class. She has middle class aspirations but almost all her friends are working class. I'm from a working class background but my lifestyle is middle class. Angie has always made a beeline for working class children and those who have been abused or fostered – they seem to be able to recognise it instinctively in other children. Perhaps it's also about being an outsider or different in some important way.

Effect on your relationship with the co-parent

We weren't a couple when Angie moved in with us, although my ex-partner had made a commitment to help bring her up for the first five years. I think if we had been trying to have a relationship and sex life, it would have been very difficult. You have to take turns in child care to give each other a break. We were able to give each other a weekend off but I don't know how we would have found enough time to be alone together.

We decided to live separately after five years, which was difficult for Angie. However, my ex has remained strongly committed to Angie and lives nearby.

I haven't found it easy to have relationships after having Angie, but then, it wasn't that easy before – it's probably not her fault!

Post-adoption support

Our social worker has remained in touch and we have become friends. She has been a great support and done things way above the call of duty.

Some of Angie's social workers in the early days were really bad. One told her that her father, who was convicted of sexually abusing her sister and making her pregnant, loved her and that was how he showed his love.

Resources

I went to some social services lectures, which were really useful. One of them showed some brain scans of children who had been abused which showed very little neural activity in some areas before they were adopted. After a year or so of nurturing, they showed how those areas of the brain were active again. It's amazing that we can help with love and care to literally light up a child's life again and that it would show so physiologically. The change all round can be quite miraculous.

Final thoughts

Overall, I would say for everything you put in, and you have to put in a lot, you get ten times back. Adopting Angie has added enormously to my life. It is very well worth doing and I don't mean that from a do-gooding perspective. You learn an enormous amount about yourself. I have a huge respect for Angie and have learned so much from her. A child's ability to go through so many bad experiences and to go on being willing to trust and love is deeply moving. You get so much love back. It has been a life-enhancing experience for me. It opens your heart.

And the relationship goes on. Angie talks about having children and maybe adopting one day.

18

Laurent and Goudarz

Goudarz is 32 and Laurent is 31. Goudarz is the director of a marketing agency and Laurent works in finance. They have been together for nearly ten years. Laurent was born in France and Goudarz is Indian of Iranian descent. They met in the United States while they were at university. Before deciding to adopt, they provided lodgings to homeless gay teenagers through the Albert Kennedy Trust. They have now adopted two boys aged two and three.

Why did you decide to adopt?

We both love children, and talked about having our own kids hardly a year into our relationship. At that time, it was more of a wish than something we ever believed could happen. When we first moved to the UK, this started becoming a possibility.

Round about the time we both decided to go ahead and apply, we started feeling paternal – there's no other way to describe it. We distinctly felt like we were ready.

What experience did you have of children beforehand?

Nothing significant. We'd both looked after nephews or nieces, friends' kids and half-siblings a bit.

How did you decide on the adoption agency you chose?

We called a number of local authorities – more than 20 – and only a handful of them seemed willing to take us on. Most of them turned us down, saying that they did not have children who matched our racial mix, though each rejection made us doubt whether that was being used as an excuse to stop a gay couple from adopting. However, I must say that later we met gay adoptive couples from some of the local authorities that had turned us down, so I guess it might not have been homophobia after all – at least not in all cases.

Of the three to four that seemed willing to work with us, an adoption charity was definitely the most positive. I remember talking to a social worker who said, 'There is homophobia in the system and so you need someone who is willing to fight for your rights. We most definitely will do everything in our power to ensure that you are not treated any differently.' That stuck in my mind, and definitely made a very good first impression. Hence we chose the adoption charity.

What was your experience of the preparation course?

It was surprisingly helpful. The instructors were really friendly. They were not exactly prepared for a gay couple on the course, and that was only visible at times when they'd have handouts that said "mother and father" or similar small stuff. However, they definitely treated us no differently than anyone else. In fact, I could distinctly sense one of them becoming quite fond of us through the four-day period. Even after the course she's always made a point of coming over and talking to us at other events organised by our agency.

How did you decide on your preference, for example, adopting siblings, or the ages and sex of children?

We were asked about it by one of the social workers who visited us the first time, and we hadn't really been prepared for the question. However, luckily, we both said the same things, more or less, with regards to ages and sex.

We had talked about wanting a big family with two or three kids, and had discussed that bit earlier. We felt that it made sense to adopt siblings rather than one at a time, as that way we would be able to take on "hard to place" kids, and at the same time not be instrumental in siblings being split because nobody wanted to take on two or three at a time. On the flip side, we thought it would also work in our favour because we'd have less competition, per se.

What was your experience of the home study?

It was relatively painless. Our social worker was nothing short of brilliant. It felt like having free therapy at times! In time, she turned into more of a good friend, even part of the family, rather than being just a social worker, and we can feel too that she is extremely fond of us, as we're her first gay adoptive couple.

Also, we'd been through a similar vetting process before we started providing supported lodgings to homeless gay teenagers via the Albert Kennedy Trust, so we were quite used to the nature of questions being asked and the process of evaluation, in many ways.

If anything, this process felt more streamlined even though it was more in-depth, largely due to the more stringent government guidelines surrounding adoption and our social worker's efficiency at her job.

What was your experience of the adoption panel?

The adoption panel felt much more unnerving than we had expected. Perhaps it was the realisation that so much was riding on it, or just the experience of having 12 strangers peering down a table at you, asking you questions that could determine the rest of your life!

The questions they asked us were all very valid – how we planned to take time off from work, how we'd handle family acceptance issues – nothing that they would not have asked any other couple, really.

What advice would you give to anyone going through these stages?

Be honest with yourself and be honest with the social workers. Social workers make a living off reading people, and if they think you're hiding something, they'll delay the process until they're satisfied that you're not a liability.

If you think you're not ready, or have doubts, talk to other people, don't think you're alone in this.

And most importantly, don't worry about society. Children need good parents, so don't let your worries about society's reaction hinder your desire and ability to give a child a loving, caring home – we've done it, and the reactions, even from strangers, and our kids' church-funded school, has been brilliant!

What was your experience of finding a match?

That, to me, was the most frustrating and difficult part of the process. It felt like we were ready and had to wait for no real reason.

It was our first experience outside of the super-efficient workings of a charity and inside the super-inefficient world of local authority social services. We'd find children we thought were a good match in *Be My Parent* and *Children Who Wait*, and send our one-page profile to the family-finders, and then wait weeks to hear back. We felt like it was beyond ridiculous that anyone could take three weeks to read one page and decide whether or not we were to be considered.

At this stage, we once again did feel there might be systemic homophobia holding us back, and our social worker hinted at times that her conversations with some family-finders led her to think that, but we don't know for sure, and we never pushed really, as this bit is just completely out of our hands – if you push, the social worker can always just give some generic excuse like, 'You're not the best match', and we're in no position to question that. Also, you never want to rock the boat in case they sincerely did not feel we were the right match for that child but might think we were suitable for another.

In hindsight, the few months didn't really matter, especially when I consider now that I have 18 years to look forward to with my boys, but I do think at times that had social workers got their act together quicker, our boys might have been with us six months earlier, and we might have got to see them learn to walk, etc. But who can tell?

Our social worker always told me, 'The right child for you is out there. You just need to wait for the time when it is meant to be.'

Please describe the children you have adopted

Two boys aged two and three (as of the time of adopting). They are blood brothers from the same two parents. They are in perfect condition, health-wise and developmentally (touch wood!).

What was your experience of meeting the boys?

By the time we met the boys, we had previously seen pictures of both of them, read a very detailed history of their backgrounds before care, met their social worker, and also met with their foster carer. That last bit was really useful, as we had a three-hour discussion with her in her house while the children were away, in which she went through all their routines, their likes/dislikes, their characters, etc. We were very lucky that we got along very well with her and received very useful information from this.

We had also prepared a book for the children with some photographs of the two of us, in regular everyday clothes, with simple texts like 'This is where Papa cooks', or 'This is where Daddy works'. As soon as we passed the matching panel, the foster carer told them about us, and showed them these photographs and a simple video of us saying hello.

So, by the time we actually met, both adopters and adoptees knew about each other to quite a large extent. This didn't stop us from being very nervous: I remember holding my partner's hand on the way to meeting the boys and thinking, 'This is the start of a new chapter in our life'.

During the introduction week, however, there was no time to really worry about things any more: we were too tired from all the excitement to have time for anything but sleep once the children were back with their foster carer!

What was it like in the first stages of settling in as a family?

The very first morning the boys woke up at home, we saw that they were developing chickenpox…a real baptism by fire! So the first week was just spent nursing them. In a way this helped us bond, as it showed them we were there for them and would take care of their health.

For the first few weeks, we really let nobody from the extended family and/or friends come to visit us. This allowed the boys to really understand the dynamics of their new family and not swamp them with new faces. Everybody understood and respected our need for privacy during those initial weeks.

What emotional and behavioural issues have you dealt with?

Nothing out of the ordinary for children their age. At the start of the settling-in process, we had to deal with more challenging behaviour, mostly because the boys didn't really know where our boundaries were, and kept testing how far they could go. But this settled down quickly with clear rules.

Have you had any contact with birth parents and family – what was that like?

We lobbied our social workers really hard to be able to meet with the birth mother. The main reason was that we had very limited information on her, in particular, no photographs of her to show the boys when they grow up. It was again a meeting that made us both very anxious beforehand, but will prove valuable in time. We were able to get pictures of her, cards that she wants us to give them on their 16th birthdays, a short video saying that she wants them to come and meet her when they grow up, an explanation of who chose their names, a detailed run-down on diseases running in the family, etc.

We also got a lot more clarification on the circumstances surrounding their being placed in care; we found that there were some substantial errors in the records held by social services.

We also met with their half-siblings. This was very touching, in particular, seeing how their half-brother resembles our older son. There again, those pictures and clarifications on the family background have proved much more illuminating than any paperwork could. We would recommend all adopters to go for contact with the birth family whenever feasible, despite the stress and anxiety this might cause.

What has been your experience of dealing with the following?

School

This went quite smoothly. We basically chose the school that was closest to us, which happened to be a Church of England school. Despite the fact that we're both atheist, we felt that the staff at the school were very warm and welcoming. We would recommend that you visit the principal and the teachers who will be involved in your child's day-to-day care. Just by seeing their reaction when realising that you're a gay or lesbian couple will give you a good idea of whether this will be an issue or not. Also, remember to ask if they have any other gay parents in the school.

Friends and family

Friends and family who had no problems with us being gay proved just as much at ease with us adopting; in many instances they were not that surprised that we decided to go down that route, and had a lot of time to adjust to any misgivings between the time we first formulated the idea and the time we actually got the children placed with us.

Unfortunately, family members who disagreed with our relationship have continued to show disapproval and made their objections very clear to us adopting.

I would say you should always explain calmly any misgivings about adoption or gay parenting when you encounter it, but don't bother to try and reason with pure homophobic remarks.

Discussing your sexuality with the children

Our children have accepted very quickly that our family is composed of two dads and do not find anything unusual in this. We've connected with other gay adopters via the New Family Social web page and regularly go to their monthly meetings. This has made a huge difference, as our children are now friends with other children who also have gay parents.

Ethnicity

This was one of the most frustrating things in the process. While the idea of placing children with parents of the same racial/cultural background makes sense, it is often pushed to an absurd level by social workers. Some children have such unique backgrounds that it is unlikely any one set of parents could tick all boxes. For example, I remember the case of this boy whom we had enquired about. He was a mix of White European, Iranian and African backgrounds. The social worker acknowledged that me (white) and my partner (Indian of Iranian descent) were a close match, but as we were missing any African connection, she would continue searching for parents. It is quite enraging realising that through such categorisation of children, mixed-heritage children end up stuck in care for so much longer than purely white children, for example.

Religion

Again, the policy of placing children with parents of the same religion might make sense in theory, but in practice this is often a hurdle for gay men. The stance of most religions on homosexuality means that a lot of gay men do not have a strong affiliation with a religious doctrine. However, social services will label children (even babies) as "Muslim", "Sikh", "Hindu", etc, as if toddlers have deeply-held religious identities. Getting past the hurdle of race only to be told that you're not from the right religion is very frustrating.

Children who have been abused – acting out patterns of abuse

It is always difficult to know, once you have children, what's normal acting-out behaviour, and what's caused by previous experiences of neglect/abuse. You have to watch out for not over-reading every little tantrum as a reflection of their past, as otherwise they will pick on that and play this against you. For example, there was a time when our oldest one genuinely missed his foster carer, and was acting out over it. After a while, however, he started to use the 'I'm missing Andy' as a standard excuse to misbehaviour, knowing that we usually would console him rather than scold him if he said that.

Experience of social services

When you're in the process, you never want to rock the boat. You've dreamt for so long about having a child, and have gone through such an invasive scrutiny from social services that (especially towards the end) you really don't want to jeopardise anything by complaining. It's very important that when things go wrong, you have someone inside the system that can be your advocate, ideally your own social worker. For this reason, it is very important to really scout for the appropriate adoption agency before starting the process. Once you're in it, it's often a terrible headache if tensions arise. From discussion with other gay adopters, it seems that local authorities are much more ineffectual and homophobic than independent adoption agencies.

The foster family

Don't forget that they have a vested interest in getting along with you. After all, they're not allowed to derail a placement (though some will). So, if you encounter problems, make them realise that, within a few weeks, you will be the ones taking care of the children, with or without their approval, and that the child's interests will be best served if everybody co-operates.

19

Sarah and Georgina

Sarah and Georgina are both white British; Sarah is 47 and Georgina is 40. They have been together since 2001 and had a civil partnership in 2006. Georgina works full-time as a ward manager in a coronary care unit. Sarah has a PhD and worked as a policy writer before giving up work to try her hand at creative writing. She hopes to combine this with looking after their child. Sarah and Georgina have adopted a three-year-old boy who is of dual heritage. Sarah tells their story.

Why did you decide to adopt?

This was always our first choice. We were quite certain that we did not want to complicate our relationship by involving a man in our desire to be parents. We are also very much opposed to the idea of anonymous donor insemination.

What experience did you have of children beforehand?

I have two nieces (now aged 18 and 20) and we have many friends with children. I also used to work as a private tutor (in English) for teenagers.

How did you decide on the adoption agency you chose?

We initially approached our local borough council and the surrounding boroughs but they all told us that they were not seeking white adopters. We contacted a few other boroughs, but they said they would only be interested in us if we would consider adopting a sibling group. I also spoke to a woman working for a charity, who was very unhelpful and a little rude (I suspect that this was because I said we were a lesbian couple). We put our plans on hold for a couple of years and then contacted our local borough council to see if things had changed and, thankfully, they were happy to approve us.

What was your experience of the preparation course?

Very good, with a lot of advice that we have made use of.

How did you decide on your preference, e.g. adopting siblings, or the ages and sex of children?

We decided that we would like to adopt a little girl under the age of three, but fell in love with a little boy who was nearly four!

What was your experience of the home study?

Although we felt that a lot of the "homework" was patronising and pointless, we felt very comfortable with our social worker. She was very friendly and supportive and, being a mother herself, was not under the illusion that anyone can be the perfect parent.

What was your experience of the adoption panel?

Generally, we were treated very well. At the approval panel we were questioned about why we wanted to adopt a dual heritage child, and we had to point out that we did not necessarily "want" to adopt a dual heritage child, but had discussed the possibility with our social worker after she broached the subject, which is why we were approved for a white or dual heritage child. The reaction of certain members of the panel showed that ethnicity is still a touchy subject for some professionals. Our matching panel was a very positive experience.

What advice would you give to anyone going through these stages?

Be patient, have someone to talk to and think about the children who are waiting to be adopted.

What was your experience of finding a match?

We were shocked to discover that even though there were plenty of children who seemed to be a suitable match, we were required to do all the chasing, almost as if we were competing in some sort of competition where we had to overcome obstacles to get the prize. Having spoken to other adopters, we are confident that this had nothing to do with our sexuality but is the result of a system that largely fails adopters and children in care. Having said that, we were very impressed with the local authority once they had decided that we were a good match for the little boy who is now our son.

What was your experience of meeting him?

This was handled very well. We met his foster carers for a chat a few weeks before we met our son, so they were able to give us a more rounded picture. We met our son for the first time at a family centre and were left alone with him for about an hour, which meant that we did not feel as if we were being watched and judged (although we were later told that the foster carers and social worker had kept checking on us through the window in the door!).

What was it like in the first stages of settling in as a family?

Our son had been very well prepared and, although he was only three, seemed to have a good grasp of the idea that he was now going to live with his forever family.

What emotional and behavioural issues have you dealt with?

Our son had been with his foster carers for about two-and-a-half years and was very happy with them. Our biggest challenge has been trying to help him come to terms with the fact that he is now living with us, but will still be able to stay in touch with his foster family. Other than that, he is a well balanced little boy and, because he was removed from his birth family when he was 18 months old, he has no clear memory of his early neglect and injuries.

Have you had any contact with birth parents and family – what was that like?

None. Although we are willing to keep in touch via social services, the birth family has not made much effort. In our son's "keep box" we have a letter written by his aunt, in which she expresses her sadness at our son being taken into care and says that she wants to maintain contact. It seems that she has made no effort since then, but she was only 17 at the time of writing the letter and probably very confused. We have decided to write to her now that she is a little older to see if she would like to have letterbox contact.

What has been your experience of dealing with the following?

School

Our son is at pre-school and we have had no problems with the teachers.

Friends and family

I think that when we discussed with friends and family our desire to adopt, their reaction was the same as if we were a straight couple, i.e. generally supportive and encouraging, with one or two people who could not understand why we did not want our "own" children (even if they never actually said this).

Discussing your sexuality with the children

All he understands at the moment is that some children have a mummy and a daddy, some have just a mummy, some have two mummies, etc. We will deal with any issues relating to our sexuality as they arise.

Race

Our son's birth mother is "mixed race" (white father, black mother), but at the moment this means very little to our son, especially as he looks very white, so he has not even asked the usual question: 'Why am I a different colour to you?' He has photos of several members of his mother's family, so I'm sure the subject of race will crop up when he is older. One of the main reasons that we were considered a suitable match is the area in which we live, which is culturally diverse.

Religion

We are not at all religious, although we have friends and acquaintances who are (mostly Christian and Muslim). We took our son to a carol service on Christmas Eve and will do so on other occasions. We feel that as he grows up he should be free to make his own decisions about religion and we would support him.

Drug addiction

Both birth parents are addicted to drugs, although our son did not have any symptoms of withdrawal after birth. Obviously, when he is older we will discuss the fact that his parents are addicts.

Dealing with homophobia

This has never really been a problem, either before or after we became parents. I'm sure that many people have rather negative views about gay parents, but we have been overwhelmed by the support from everyone in our life. We accept that as a family we will inevitably be subjected to homophobia at some point, which we will deal with as and when it happens.

Social services

Although we are appalled by the slowness and lack of sense that seems to run through the whole system, we have never felt the need to complain about individual social workers.

The foster family

We began by thinking that the foster mum and dad were brilliant, but have come to realise that this is just what they want everyone to think! In reality, our son had a very bad diet, lack of stimulation, etc. However, because they were the only family he knew before us, we have agreed to keep in touch for the sake of our son.

Making a photo album/video to introduce yourselves to the child

The album included photos of my partner and me, our families, the house and garden, our car, etc. We were also asked to do a recording of each of us reading a bedtime story so that our son could become accustomed to our voices.

Playing one parent off against another

Our son occasionally tries to do this, but we just carry on as normal and he soon gets bored and is back to his usual loving self.

Setting boundaries

Our son knows that 'no means no' and that he is expected to behave in a certain way, i.e. does not answer back, comes to the table when we ask him to, etc. We also have a lot of fun and he spends most of the day giggling and chattering non-stop.

Leave from work, employers' and colleague's attitudes

I was already working from home and intend to give up work for a while. My partner has taken about six months' adoption leave and although she is very much missed at work, has had a great deal of support.

Attachment disorder

Our son has attached very quickly and we cannot imagine life without him.

Class

At the risk of sounding like an awful snob, my partner and I are university-educated and middle class, while the foster family is quite working class. Our son has come from an environment where the (huge) TV was constantly switched on, *The Sun* was the paper of choice, he ate ready meals (often in front of the TV), and was actually treated as if he was still a little toddler. However, because of his age he has adapted very well to our way of life.

Post-adoption support

Very good – we have an excellent social worker.

20

Endpiece

It will be interesting to write another book in ten years' time from the perspective of children adopted by the gay men and lesbians featured in this book. Here we feature the thoughts of a 21-year-old woman who was adopted by a lesbian. Her story is thought-provoking and heart-warming.

Many lesbians saved my life
Jennie Alderson

Before I met Mum and Sue, social services hadn't talked to me about going to live with lesbians (I was eight years old then). But I had already told them I didn't want a dad. I had had bad experiences with my own dad and didn't want another one. I also had lived with two different families who were going to adopt me, but neither of them worked out and they both had a mum and dad and another child in the family. So I felt safe with two mums. It wasn't exactly two mums – my mum was Lynn and Sue wasn't the same as a mum, though she wasn't a dad either, so we eventually worked out that I called her my co-parent.

Anyway, before we met, they sent me a book with pictures about their family and I could see who they were, and all the cats and where they lived. I thought, yeah, I really want to go and live there. I still have the book, I used to love looking at it. I wouldn't have known what a lesbian was, but Mum says that when I first looked around the house and saw her big bed, I asked, 'Who do you sleep with?'

Mostly, I just really wanted to get out of foster care, I had been in care one way or another since I was four and I wasn't happy. I still had my birth mum whom I saw sometimes; she died after I was adopted. But there was a court case where she tried to stop the adoption and I was angry about that because I really wanted to be adopted. I don't think I knew at the time that the case was about Lynn and Sue being lesbians, they didn't tell me everything then. But we won the case and the adoption went ahead. To me, it was no big deal that they were lesbians, it's never been a big problem.

At school, when I was about 10, there was one time when another kid said something about my mum being a lesbian, and I said she wasn't and when I told my mum about it she asked why I said that, and I said because you aren't sleeping with anyone. She explained about being a lesbian to me then and that she was still one even if she wasn't having a relationship at the time. Even though she and Sue stopped being together in that way, Sue has always lived with or near us and stayed my co-parent.

Later on, when I met another girl who had a lesbian mother, we compared notes. She wasn't adopted, but we thought that there were lots of similar things about them, for example, they all seem to have Everything but the Girl and Massive Attack and Tracey Chapman records somewhere in their collections. Although her mum had, at that time, a no.1 skinhead haircut and wore axes, etc, and my mum wasn't like that. I suppose it would have been harder for me if she had been. When my friends came round they might ask, and I never had a problem saying that she was a lesbian, although I never talked about it much. But if you were just in the street or something you wouldn't really know, although she never shaved her legs and sometimes didn't wear a bra. Anyway, I think it drew us together, my friend and I, and we've stayed close friends.

Another girl came up to me at secondary school and said, 'Your mum is like mine'. But we live in Hebden Bridge and there's a lot of people with easygoing, hippie views here and really no one is that bothered. If friends asked me why I had two mums, I'd say because I didn't want a dad.

I loved having lots of aunties. We didn't have a lot of men around, but I had lots of my mum's friends and could pick who I wanted to be close to. Now that I am an adult, there are men in my life and I do have relationships with them. But I felt that in growing up I was allowed to be who I wanted to be, I never felt I had to be like my mum or a lesbian. I had a safe place in which to grow up into me. I felt loved and wanted. My mate feels the same and we both think that we have lots of friends who are girls too, that that's important to us. And sometimes we go to the women's disco even though we aren't lesbians. Also, that perhaps having been brought up by strong feminist women, we are good at spotting crap in men and we won't put up with it. And we know more about women's rights.

What was important was that my mum was a good mum to me, she is a great mum and we just fitted right away, we bonded. I don't think that there is any problem about having a lesbian mum. I was going to start writing my autobiography and I thought of calling it *Many Lesbians Saved My Life*. It's true.

(This first appeared in *Be My Parent*, May 2009.)

References

Bailey JM, Bobrow D, Wolfe M and Mikach S (1995) 'Sexual orientation of adult sons of gay fathers', *Developmental Psychology*, 31, pp. 124–129

Barrett H and Tasker F (2001) 'Growing up with a gay parent: views of 101 gay fathers on their sons' and daughters' experiences', *Educational and Child Psychology*, 18, pp. 62–77

Brooks D and Goldberg S (2001) 'Gay and lesbian adoptive and foster care placements: can they meet the needs of waiting children?', *Social Work*, 46:2, pp. 147–157

Brown HC (1991) 'Competent child-focused practice: working with lesbian and gay carers', *Adoption & Fostering*, 15:2, pp. 11– 17

Cosis-Brown H and Cocker C (2008) 'Lesbian and gay fostering and adoption: out of the closet, into the mainstream?', *Adoption & Fostering*, 32:4, pp. 19–30

Gartrell N, Deck A, Rodas C, Peyser H and Banks A (2005) 'The National Lesbian Family Study: 4. Interviews with the 10-year-old children', *American Journal of Orthopsychiatry*, 75:4, pp. 518–524

Golombok S and Tasker F (1996) 'Do parents influence the sexual orientation of their children? Findings from a longitudinal study of lesbian families', *Developmental Psychology*, 32:1, pp. 3–11

Howard J and Freundlich M (2008) *Expanding Resources for Waiting Children II: Eliminating legal and practice barriers to gay and lesbian adoption from foster care*, Evan B Donaldson Adoption Institute, accessed at www.adoptioninstitute.org/research/2008_09_expand_resources.php

Huggins SL (1989) 'A comparative study of self-esteem of adolescent children of divorced lesbian mothers and divorced heterosexual mothers', in Bozett FW (ed) *Homosexuality and the Family*, New York, NY: Harrington Park Press, pp. 123–135

Mallon G (2004) *Gay Men Choosing Parenthood*, New York, NY: Columbia University Press

Mallon G and Betts B (2005) *Recruiting, Assessing and Supporting Lesbian and Gay Carers and Adopters*, London: BAAF

McCann D and Delmonte H (2005) 'Lesbian and gay parenting: babes in arms or babes in the woods?,' *Sexual and Relationship Therapy*, 20:3, pp. 333–347

Patterson CJ (2009) *Lesbian and Gay Parenting*, accessed at www.apa.org/pi/lgbc/publications/lgpconclusion.html

Rosenfeld MJ (2007) *Nontraditional Families and Childhood Progress Through School*, American Sociological Association, accessed at www.allacademic.com//meta/p_mla_apa_research_citation/1/8/3/6/4/pages183640/p183640-1.php

Scallen RM (1981) 'An investigation of paternal attitudes and behaviours in homosexual and heterosexual fathers', *Dissertation Abstracts International*, 42, pp. 3809-B

Tasker F (2005) 'Lesbian mothers, gay fathers and their children: a review', *Journal of Developmental and Behavioral Pediatrics*, 26, pp. 224–240

Tasker F and Bellamy C (2007) 'Reviewing lesbian and gay adoption and foster care: the developmental outcomes for children', *Family Law*, 37, pp. 473–570

Tasker F and Golombok S (1997) *Growing up in a Lesbian Family: Effects on child development*, New York, NY: Guilford Press

Useful organisations

British Association for Adoption & Fostering
Saffron House
6–10 Kirby Street
London EC1N 8TS
Tel: 020 7421 2600
www.baaf.org.uk
The leading UK charity working for children separated from their birth families. It has an advice line and publishes a wide range of books on adoption, from personal accounts to guides for social workers. Visit the website for a database of adoption agencies and information about adoption legislation. BAAF publishes *Be My Parent*, a family-finding newspaper and website which feature children needing adoption (see www.bemyparent.org.uk).

BAAF also operates the Adoption Register for England and Wales (see www.adoptionregister.org.uk) and the Independent Review Mechanism (see www.irm-adoption.org.uk).

BAAF Scotland
113 Rose Street
Edinburgh EH2 3DT
Tel: 0131 226 9270

BAAF Cymru
7 Cleeve House
Lambourne Crescent
Cardiff CF14 5GP
Tel: 02920 761155

BAAF Northern Ireland
Botanic House
1–5 Botanic Avenue
Belfast BT7 1JG
Tel: 028 9031 5494

Adoption UK
46 The Green
South Bar Street
Banbury OX16 9AB
Helpline: 0844 848 7900
www.adoptionuk.org
Adoption UK was established in 1971 and is a national self-help
group run by and for adoptive parents and foster carers, offering
support before, during and after adoption. It has a lively message
board specifically for gay men and lesbians going through the
process of adoption. It publishes *Adoption Today*, a bimonthly which
includes news, reports and features and *Children Who Wait*, a
monthly, which provides profiles of children needing adoption.

PACE Family Support Service
34 Hartham Road
London N7 9LJ
Tel: 020 7700 1323
www.pacehealth.org.uk
An organisation which offers support, advice and counselling to
lesbian and gay parents. This includes workshops, couple
counselling, a helpline and a 12-week support group.

Adoption Information Line

Freephone: 0800 783 4086

www.adoption.org.uk

This provides advice and information to the general public about adoption.

Adults Affected by Adoption – Norcap

112 Church Road

Wheatley

Oxon OX33 1LU

Tel: 01865 875000

www.norcap.org.uk

Offers support, counselling and an intermediary service for tracing birth relatives.

The D'Arcy Lainey Foundation

Unit 29 Hillier Road

Devizes

Wiltshire SN10 2FB

Tel: 01380 727935

www.dalafo.co.uk

The D'Arcy Lainey Foundation (DALAFO) is a national, voluntary, not-for-profit organisation working with and for LGBT families. It provides support, guidance and social activities to all LGBT families and those wishing to start a family, and manages the national project, Pink Parents.

Parentline Plus

520 Highgate Studios

53–79 Highgate Road

London NW5 1TL

Helpline: 0808 800 2222 (24 hours a day, every day)

Textphone: 0800 783 6783

www.parentlineplus.org.uk/

Offers support to anyone parenting a child, the child's parents, step-parents, grandparents and foster parents. Runs free telephone and email helplines, parenting courses and offers information leaflets.

Stonewall
Tower Building
York Road
London SE1 7NX
Tel: 0800 050 2020
www.stonewall.org.uk/
The campaigning group for lesbians, gay men and bisexuals has a wealth of information available for parents on its website.

YoungMinds Parents' Helpline
Tel: 0800 018 2138
www.youngminds.org.uk/parents/more-about-the-parents-information-service/what-is-the-parents-information-service
A telephone service that gives information to anyone concerned with the mental health of a child.

Out for our Children
www.outforourchildren.co.uk
A group of London lesbian parents producing books and resources that reflect the lives and family experiences of children with lesbian parents.

Support groups

New Family Social
www.newfamilysocial.co.uk
A UK-wide charity working for lesbian and gay adopters and their children, with a large network of support and regular social activities. New Family Social links members with other families in their area, and provides children with opportunities to build friendships with other adopted children of gay and lesbian parents. Membership is also open to those who have yet to find an agency, and offers access to a thriving online community with a 24-hour, members-only message board for sharing advice, knowledge and support. A library of materials relevant to gay and lesbian adoption is also available. New Family Social is pro-active with media work,

and is developing service provision for adoption teams: research, training, family-finding, access to information and expertise.

OASIS

Helpline: 0870 241 7069
www.adoptionoverseas.org
This is a UK-based voluntary support group for people who wish to adopt, or who have already adopted, children from overseas.

Gay Dads Scotland

PO Box 23825
Edinburgh City EH3 6UB
Tel: 07791 188742
www.gaydadsscotland.org.uk/
Social and support group for gay fathers living in Scotland. The website has links to research articles that examine the effects on children on being brought up by lesbian, gay or bisexual parents.

Proud 2B Parents

Tel: 0161 2260162
Email: matt_1982_roberts@hotmail.com
An LGBT parents group based in Manchester, which meets every 4th Saturday of the month at Alexandra Park Play Centre. It is the first gay parents group in the UK to be supported by Sure Start.

Northern Support Group

Tel: 07949 254620
Email: northernsupportgroup@hotmail.co.uk
www.nsgroup.org.uk
This group meets mainly in Manchester, but also in Leeds, Bradford and Sheffield, to offer support and advice to any lesbians or gay men who are thinking about or going through the process of fostering or adoption. The group provides a crèche and a space in which people can chat, share stories and advice.

Rainbow Families

Tel: 07903 397108
Email: rainbow_families@hotmail.com
Rainbow Families aims to provide support and information for lesbian and bisexual women who are parents or who want to become parents. It is a voluntary organisation and operates a monthly drop-in close to Manchester city centre. Contact the group if you would like to attend one of their events or attend a drop-in session.

Useful websites

Adoption-Net

www.adoption-net.co.uk/
This website provides information for anyone thinking about adoption.

BAAF

www.baaf.org.uk
BAAF's website has a wealth of information on adoption.

Be My Parent

www.bemyparent.org.uk
Contains information and is also a family-finding website.

Directgov

www.direct.gov.uk/en/Parents/Adoptionfosteringandchildrenincare/index.htm
This is the government's information site for adoption and fostering.

Proud Parenting

www.proudparenting.com/
An American website aimed at gay parents with news and helpful information.

Useful reading

Books for adults

These books have been recommended by gay men and lesbians who were interviewed for this book.

Turan Ali (1996) *We Are Family: Testimonies of lesbian and gay parents*, London: Continuum

Caroline Archer (1999) *First Steps in Parenting a Child who Hurts: Tiddlers and toddlers*, London and Philadelphia: Jessica Kingsley Publishers

Caroline Archer (1999) *Next Steps in Parenting a Child who Hurts: Tykes and teens*, London and Philadelphia: Jessica Kingsley Publishers

Katherine Arnup (1995) *Lesbian Parenting: Living with pride and prejudice*, Charlottetown, PEI: Gynergy Books

Stephanie A Brill (2001) *The Queer Parent's Primer: A lesbian and gay families' guide to navigating the straight world*, Oakland, CA: New Harbinger Publications

Vera Fahlberg (1994) *A Child's Journey through Placement*, London: BAAF

Be my parent
www.bemyparent.org.uk

Thousands of children in the UK are waiting for an adoptive or permanent foster family...

Could you be that family?

To look at the profiles of some of these children, find out if adoption or fostering is for you, or to subscribe to **Be My Parent**, visit **www.bemyparent.org.uk** or call **020 7421 2666.**

Be My Parent is a family-finding service provided by the British Association for Adoption & Fostering which brings waiting children and families together through a website and a monthly colour newspaper.

BAAF
ADOPTION & FOSTERING

LOTTERY FUNDED | BIG LOTTERY FUND

British Association for Adoption and Fostering is a registered charity no. 275689 (England and Wales) and SC039337 (Scotland)

Abigail Garner (2004) *Families Like Mine: Children of gay parents tell it like it is*, New York, NY: HarperCollins

Deborah Glazer and Jack Drescher (2001) *Gay and Lesbian Parenting*, Kirkwood, NY: Harrington Park Press

Perlita Harris (2006) *In Search of Belonging: Reflections by transracially adopted people*, London: BAAF

Stephan Hicks, Stephen McDermott and Janet McDermott (eds) (1999) *Lesbian and Gay Fostering and Adoption: Extraordinary yet ordinary*, London and Philadelphia: Jessica Kingsley Publishers

Daniel A Hughes (2006) *Building the Bonds of Attachment*, Lanham, MD: Jason Aronson Publishers

Jenifer Lord (2008) *Adopting a Child: A guide for people interested in adoption*, London: BAAF

Gerald Mallon and Bridget Betts (2005) *Recruiting, Assessing and Supporting Lesbian and Gay Carers and Adopters*, London: BAAF

April Martin (1993) *The Lesbian and Gay Parenting Handbook: Creating and raising our families*, New York, NY: HarperPerennial

April Martin (1994) *The Guide to Lesbian and Gay Parenting*, London: Rivers Orham Press

KJ McGarry (2003) *Fatherhood for Gay Men: An emotional and practical guide to becoming a gay dad*, Binghampton, NJ: Haworth Press

Ann Morris (1999) *The Adoption Experience: Families who give children a second chance*, London and Philadephia: Jessica Kingsley Publishers

Marjorie Morrison (2007) *Talking about Adoption to your Adopted Child: A guide for parents by adoption* (4th edn), London: BAAF

Lisa Saffron (2001) *It's a Family Affair: The complete lesbian parenting book*, London: Diva Press

Amy Neil Salter (2006) *The Adopter's Handbook: Information, resources and services for adoptive parents* (3rd edn), London: BAAF

Nancy Verrier (1993) *The Primal Wound: Understanding the adopted child*, Lafayette, CA: Verrier Publications

Brett Webb-Mitchell (2007) *On Being a Gay Parent*, New York, NY: Church Publishing

Jeffrey Weeks, Brian Heaphy and Catherine Donovan (2001) *Same-Sex Intimacies: Families of choice and other life experiments*, London: Routledge

Our Story series

The Our Story series, published by BAAF, provides an insight into the highs and lows of adoption through the real-life experiences of a wide range of families.

Maria James (2006) *An Adoption Diary: A couple's journey from infertility to parenthood*

Julia Wise (2007) *Flying Solo: A single parent's adoption story*

Nathalie Seymour (2007) *In Black and White: The story of an open transracial adoption*

Karen Carr (2007) *Adoption Undone: A painful story of an adoption breakdown*

Robert Marsden (2008) *The Family Business: The story of a family's adoption of a boy with cerebral palsy*

Ruth and Ed Royce (2008) *Together in Time: How creative therapies helped a family who adopted two boys with attachment difficulties*

Laurel Ashton (2008) *Take Two: A story about confronting infertility, exploring alternatives and adopting two babies*

Books for children

Hedi Argent (2007) *Josh and Jaz have Three Mums*, London: BAAF

Kathleen A. Chara and Paul J. Chara (2005) *A Safe Place for Caleb: An interactive book for kids, teens and adults with issues of attachment, grief, loss or early trauma*, London and Philadelphia: Jessica Kingsley Publishers

Harvey Fierstein (2002) *The Sissy Duckling*, New York, NY: Simon & Schuster

Carole Livingston (1995) *Why was I Adopted? Facts of Adoption with Love and Illustrations*, New York, NY: Citadel Press

Todd Parr (2004) *It's OK to be Different*, New York, NY: Little Brown & Co

Justin Richardson and Peter Parnell (2007) *And Tango Makes Three*, New York, NY: Simon & Schuster

Pat Thomas and Lesley Harker (2003) *A First Look at Adoption: My parents picked me!*, London: Wayland Press

Magazines and newspapers

Adoption UK's family-finding magazine, *Children Who Wait*, is published each month and features profiles of children currently looking for new families.

Be My Parent, a monthly newspaper published by BAAF, features children waiting for adoption. A website is also available at www.bemyparent.org.uk.